DOING BLACK DIGITAL HUMANITIES WITH RADICAL INTENTIONALITY

T0386435

Based on the auto-ethnographic work of a team of scholars who developed the first major Black Digital Humanities program at a research institution, this book details how to centralize Black feminist praxes of care, ethics, and Black studies in the digital humanities (DH).

In this important and timely collection, the authors Catherine Knight Steele, Jessica H. Lu, and Kevin C. Winstead—of the first team of the African American Digital Humanities Initiative—center Black scholars, Black thought, and Black studies in creating digital research and programming. Providing insight into acquiring funding, building and maintaining community, developing curricula, and establishing a national network in the field, this book moves Black persons and Black thought from the margins to the center with a set of best practices and guiding questions for scholars, students, and practitioners developing programming, creating work agreements, building radically intentional pedagogy and establishing an ethical future for Black DH.

This is essential reading for researchers, students, scholars, and practitioners working in the fields of DH and Black studies, as well as graduate students, faculty, and administrators working in humanities disciplines who are interested in forming centers, courses, and/or research programs in Black digital studies.

Catherine Knight Steele is an Associate Professor of Communication at the University of Maryland. She served as the founding director of the African American Digital Humanities Initiative and now directs the Black Communication and Technology Lab and is Co-PI for the Mellon-funded Digital Inquiry Speculation Collaboration and Optimism Network. Dr. Steele's research has been published in journals such as *Social Media + Society*, *Feminist Media Studies*, and *Television and New Media*. She is the author of the award-winning *Digital Black Feminism* (2021).

Jessica H. Lu is Associate Director of the Design Cultures & Creativity (DCC) living-learning program in the Honors College at the University of Maryland, College Park, and an Adjunct Professor in the Master's program in Engaged & Public Humanities at Georgetown University. She formerly served as a founding Postdoctoral Associate and, later, Assistant Director of the African American Digital Humanities Initiative. Dr. Lu's research has been published in *Rhetoric and Public Affairs* and *Information, Communication & Society*, while her teaching pursues care- and justice-centered approaches to digital humanities, creative language practice, and technological innovation.

Kevin C. Winstead is a Project on Rhetorics of Equity, Access, Computation, and Humanities (PREACH) Lab Postdoctoral Fellow in the School of Literature, Media, and Communication at the Georgia Institute of Technology. He formerly served as the CLIR Postdoctoral Fellow for Black Data Curation with the Center for Black Digital Research at Pennsylvania State University. Kevin was the founding Project Manager for the African American Digital Humanities Initiative. Dr. Winstead's research has been published in *Ethnic and Racial Studies*, *Sociology Compass*, and *Critical Intersections in Contemporary Curriculum & Pedagogy*. Kevin's teaching focuses on restorative learning practices, justice-centered digital studies, and critical histories.

DOING BLACK DIGITAL HUMANITIES WITH RADICAL INTENTIONALITY

A Practical Guide

Catherine Knight Steele, Jessica H. Lu, and Kevin C. Winstead

Routledge
Taylor & Francis Group

NEW YORK AND LONDON

Designed cover image: *Electric Spring*/Nettrice R. Gaskins

First published 2023
by Routledge
605 Third Avenue, New York, NY 10158

and by Routledge
4 Park Square, Milton Park, Abingdon, Oxon, OX14 4RN

Routledge is an imprint of the Taylor & Francis Group, an informa business

© 2023 Catherine Knight Steele, Jessica H. Lu and Kevin C. Winstead

The right of Catherine Knight Steele, Jessica H. Lu, and Kevin C. Winstead to be identified as authors of this work has been asserted in accordance with sections 77 and 78 of the Copyright, Designs and Patents Act 1988.

All rights reserved. No part of this book may be reprinted or reproduced or utilized in any form or by any electronic, mechanical, or other means, now known or hereafter invented, including photocopying and recording, or in any information storage or retrieval system, without permission in writing from the publishers.

Trademark notice: Product or corporate names may be trademarks or registered trademarks, and are used only for identification and explanation without intent to infringe.

ISBN: 978-1-032-28920-5 (hbk)
ISBN: 978-1-032-28723-2 (pbk)
ISBN: 978-1-003-29913-4 (ebk)

DOI: 10.4324/9781003299134

Typeset in Bembo
by SPi Technologies India Pvt Ltd (Straive)

CONTENTS

FIGURES

ACKNOWLEDGMENTS

This book was made possible by the visionary work of many folks who conceived of, funded, and supported the African American History, Culture, and Digital Humanities (AADHum) Initiative at the University of Maryland from 2015 to 2019. We are forever grateful for their work and that their vision and labor brought us together as a team.

Specifically, we thank the staff of the College of Arts and Humanities Dean's office; the Academic Technology and Administrative Operations team, especially Kathleen Cavanaugh, Nathaniel Kuhn, and Monica Milstead; and the staff of the Maryland Institute of Technology in the Humanities (MITH) who thought and worked alongside us.

We also extend our gratitude to Jovonne Bickerstaff, Justin Hosbey, Melissa Brown, Will Thomas, and Megan Fitzmaurice for their work on the project. Their dedication, wisdom, and commitment helped shape AADHum and, by extension, this manuscript.

Individually, we are grateful to the family and friends who indulged our long hours and attention to AADHum for those years. Their support nourished us and further enabled us to pay it forward to AADHum's rich, vibrant, and generous community.

Yet, the work of Black DH begins so many years before AADHum and continues to extend in the years since we left the initiative. Writing this book gave us the opportunity to be in conversation with the words, projects, and possibilities formed by Black scholars who created a field of study and provided generous examples of how to do this work with care. There are too many to list here, but we see your work and thank you for it.

Finally, we offer our thanks to the many students, scholars, visionaries, activists, and practitioners who trusted us and joined in this effort—those of you whose faces we saw so often and whose words and lessons we learned from at AADHum's events and programs. In each conversation with you, we were reminded over and over again that the work mattered—and still does. We are deeply appreciative that you allowed us this rare chance to build something new, and even more grateful that so many of you have taken up the mantle and are continuing this work in spaces and places far and wide. We hope this text provides you some measure of the support, affirmation, and insight we know you need.

Thank you to Dr. Nettrice Gaskins whose piece "electric spring" graces the cover of this book. We think it beautifully tells the story of how with intentionality, Black image, art, history, and culture can challenge our assumptions about digital technology. We also think this piece points toward the optimism of a digital humanities landscape where Black people, theories, and histories are no longer at the periphery but at the center of our work.

INTRODUCTION

Intentionally Digital, Intentionally Black

Catherine Knight Steele, Jessica H. Lu, and Kevin C. Winstead

The name for the 2018 *Intentionally Digital, Intentionally Black* conference came from a series of conversations within our team about a disconnect we had witnessed for three years. Since the hashtag #BlackLivesMatter—and the accompanying declaration—became popularized in mainstream discourse, many scholars who had never engaged in digital research before were now turning their attention to social media and digital tools as a mechanism to study online activism, harassment, violence, and racism. When folks found out that you could scrape Twitter and end up with millions of tweets for your analysis and that there were tools that could help you code data at a large scale, they were rightly intrigued. It also seemed that many scholars in digital humanities (DH) fields were, for many reasons, turning their attention to texts and data from African American history and culture—even if this had not previously been their area of expertise. In many ways, the African American History, Culture, and Digital Humanities initiative (AADHum) at the University of Maryland was born of this wave of new interest on the part of administrators and outside funders. Yet, for those who had been studying Black media and DH for years, this new interest also gave pause. Being interested in digital technology or Black culture is excellent but only when paired with the intention, training, and experience needed to move into this space with ethics and care for the people at the center of this work.

As we sat together to think about what our first national conference would be, whom it would serve, how it could feel, and how we could hold ourselves accountable, we kept circling back to intention. Work that relies upon Black culture, Black artifacts, and Black texts within DH cannot merely *happen to be* Black; it must be intentionally Black. And, work that takes up the use of digital tools or locates its sites of inquiry in digital spaces must be intentionally digital. This means it is not enough anymore for Black studies to be a periphery of DH,

DOI: 10.4324/9781003299134-1

nor can digital inquiry continue to be treated as an appendix to more traditional kinds of humanities and social science research projects, grants, and centers.

Launched in 2016, AADHum at the University of Maryland (initially called *Synergies among Digital Humanities and African American History and Culture*) guided students, faculty, and community members in their research and teaching at the intersection of African American History, culture, and DH. In the initiative's first three years, our team hosted reading groups, led training sessions, supported and sponsored research, created new courses, helped faculty update their curricula, and created a space of mentorship, support, and community for those on and off-campus. The years of programming culminated in the first national conference for Black DH, *Intentionally Digital, Intentionally Black*. As a major research institution program with private funding from the Andrew W. Mellon Foundation, AADHum's success inspired many scholars in the field to seek institutional support to create their projects across the country. Our team members went on to lead some of those projects, directing other labs, starting new research centers, creating new models of pedagogy and mentorship for undergraduates, and managing funding initiatives for other organizations.

The past few years have seen exponential growth in Black digital studies and DH. Funders from the National Endowment for the Humanities to the Andrew W. Mellon Foundation have disbursed a record number of awards at the intersection of race and technology (at the same time, long-standing mechanisms of support for scholars of color, like the Ford Foundation fellowships, are drawing to a close). Labs and institutes are now equipped with the financial support needed to start new programs, support students, and offer training in this critical area. Moreover, 2021–2022 saw a record number of tenure track positions offered in Black digital studies/humanities across the United States. Even—and, perhaps, *especially*—as the literature is multiplying due to funding and increased recognition of the area across disciplines, the field urgently needs guidance on approaching this new digital landscape with radical intentionality.

The AADHum initiative was initially funded with the promise of creating a replicable model for others to follow as they embark on this burgeoning field. Constance Crompton, Richard J. Lane, and Ray Siemens (2016) offer guides broadly on doing DH and Roopika Risam (2018) signals the impotence of crafting specific processes in post-colonial DH work. Yet, as we will argue in this text, Black DH requires its own principles and praxes that centralize the Black people, histories, and theories at the heart of our work. Too often, we assume that being good at one's research prepares us to support and steward the work of others and to do so with ethics and care. In the following chapters, we draw upon the lessons our team learned in program development and the expertise they cultivated from their work in teaching, training, and fostering community in Black DH. We insist that care is a radical practice in the academy rooted in Black feminist praxis. Through an interweaving of narrative, auto-ethnographic reflection, feminist critique, and critical analysis of artifacts, *Doing Black Digital Humanities with*

Radical Intentionality walks readers through the process of establishing and sustaining research, communities, and programming that is, both and always, intentionally digital and intentionally Black.

What Is Radial Intentionality?

Simply put, this text is for those who are *deliberate* about *changing* the relationship between research-focused centers and the communities we claim to serve. Loaded within our use of radical intentionality are terms of love, justice, and liberation. We argue that prior to adopting a practice of radical intentionality, we must first develop an ethic of radical love. As Cornel West (2011) claims, "To be human, you must bear witness to justice. Justice is what love looks like in public—to be human is to love and be loved." Channeling bell hooks (2006), we employed an "ethic of love" as the means by which we were guided to remedy the tensions at the intersection of community and the academy. As hooks says, "Working within community, whether it be sharing a project with another person, or with a larger group, we are able to experience joy in struggle." We declare and commit to radical intentionality as one way to break through the social change industrial complex of the neoliberal academy.

In that tradition, we are informed by the work of scholars such as Patricia Hill Collins (2013), who calls upon us to speak truth to power by acknowledging and pushing back against the status quo found within the power relations of the academy and grant funding processes; and, to speak truth to the people—which we interpret as creating intervening possibilities for inclusion and interdisciplinary literacy into the often-gated DH community and its methodologies. Drawing further upon Black feminist traditions, we learn lessons derived from alternative sources of knowledge production, such as those generously passed down to us through Black folklore and storytelling. We see ourselves informed by the songs of our foremothers and fathers. We write this book as our "Wade in the Water," a testimony of deliverance from humble beginnings to the other side of institutional grant work, a journey that challenged us to identify, articulate, and remain true to our principles.

So for us, radical intentionality in doing Black DH requires a deep and abiding love for the Black folks at the center of our praxis. It requires accountability to those with which we establish community. Radical intentionality prioritizes the care of Black people, Black texts and artifacts, Black histories and culture over the tools we use in DH scholarship. And finally radical intentionality challenges the status quo within institutions that would limit the possibilities and voices of those who are traditionally marginalized and maligned in academia.

Who Is Writing This Text?

This text brings the core team of the first iteration of the AADHum initiative back together to reflect upon our work in creating the vision, programming, and ethos that guided AADHum for its inaugural three years. In coming together now, three years after the conclusion of our work, the team also draws upon our experiences in starting new centers, working for funding agencies, and creating knowledge and curricula for programs in design, digital studies, and Black DH research.

Catherine Knight Steele was the founding director of the AADHum initiative. She is now an Associate Professor of Communication at the University of Maryland. She serves as the Director of the Black Communication and Technology Lab and Co-PI for the Mellon-funded Digital Inquiry Speculation Collaboration and Optimism Network (DISCO) and Director of the Graduate Certificate in Digital Studies in the Arts and Humanities. Dr. Steele has studied online Black discursive practices, Black feminism, and digital studies for over a decade. Her research has been published in multiple new media and internet studies journals, and her first monograph, *Digital Black Feminism* was published with NYU Press in 2021. Catherine came to DH from communication and media studies, having never initially considered herself a DHer. She doesn't make *things* but sees her contribution to DH as making *space* for others to build, collaborate and grow their own Black digital projects and centers. She brings a deep commitment to the critical humanistic study of digital culture and years of experience securing, reviewing, and directing externally funded DH grants and consulting on curriculum development and programming in Black DH and multiple institutions.

Jessica H. Lu is the interim Director of the Design Cultures & Creativity (DCC) living-learning program in the Honors College at the University of Maryland, College Park; an Adjunct Professor in the Master's program in Engaged & Public Humanities at Georgetown University; and, an Adjunct Professor in the Master's in Communication program at Johns Hopkins University's Advanced Academic Programs. She formerly served the AADHum initiative in a variety of capacities, first as a Graduate Assistant; later, as a Postdoctoral Associate; and, finally, as Assistant Director. As a direct result of this work, she was elected to a position on the TEI Technical Council in 2019, which she held until the end of her term in 2021. Dr. Lu's research has been published in *Rhetoric & Public Affairs* and *Information, Communication & Society*, while her teaching pursues care- and justice-centered approaches to DH, creative language practice, and technological innovation. Jessica's initial exploration of digital tools and methods was facilitated primarily through her work with AADHum; she, therefore, feels a kindred spirit among others who grow dissatisfied or disenchanted by their analog-based training and see in DH the potential for new challenges and opportunities. Ultimately, however, she is driven by a commitment to understanding and analyzing text, in all its forms. In addition to providing insights from multiple vantage points in AADHum's leadership structure, her contributions to this text ruminate on AADHum's efforts to include and nourish the most timid and digitally curious newcomers to the Black DH community through undergraduate pedagogy.

Kevin C. Winstead was a Council on Library and Information Resources (CLIR) Postdoctoral Fellow with the Center for Black Digital Research at Penn State University. This position has been recognized as part of the first nationally funded cohort at the intersection of Data Curation for African American and African Studies. He is now a Postdoctoral Fellow for the Project on Rhetorics of Equity, Access, Computation, and Humanities (PREACH) Lab at Georgia Tech, part of the Digital Inquiry Speculation Collaboration Optimism (DISCO) Network. Dr. Winstead served as the founding project manager for AADHum. At the core of his work is community, where he continues to advocate for the need for Black project managers for grant-funded projects working with Black communities, Black archives, and Black data. Kevin has established himself at the ground floor of several of the nation's emergent Black Digital Studies centers—not only AADHum, but also the Center for Black Digital Research and, now, the DISCO Network's PREACH Lab. His career has uniquely positioned him in the space where African American Studies and building DH centers collide. Kevin's book manuscript, *Sankofa Cyberculture: Black Digital Activism and Disinformation*, focuses on Black activists' cultural production in online space and foreign attempts to produce disruptive propaganda. He comes to digital studies from an ethnographic tradition, building upon the practice of decentering tools to cultivate community relationships with vulnerable populations.

We write this introduction and our conclusion together as a collective. Yet, the body of the work contains chapters, each shepherded by one of the authors so that their experiences and voice might be at the heart of the learning. While we thought together and worked in concert while writing this text, we also hope to model the trust of respecting our co-author's experiences and expertise. Rather than a collection of disparate essays curated by one editor, we write this book as a truly collaborative effort to tell the whole story, defying the temptation to present a single narrative when there are many. Each author's contributions offer an opportunity to observe and analyze AADHum's work—and its various circumstances and dynamics—from a unique vantage point. Taken together, these insights underscore the necessary collaboration that enabled AADHum's operations and made it possible for each of us to bring radical intentionality to our own distinct but interconnected scope of work.

Who Should Be Reading This Book?

There are an increasing number of conferences, convenings, and seminar courses focused on digital studies and DH across the country. The Mellon foundation disbursed awards to the University of Michigan, Purdue University, Georgia Tech, University of Maryland, Johns Hopkins, and many others in race, Black culture, and digital studies in the past couple years. At the same time, the NEH has awarded funds to numerous Historically Black Colleges and Universities (HBCUs) to start or support their curricula and centers in DH. Each of these institutions will inevitably require support and mentorship from teams of scholars who have already found success in this area. As a small sub-field, we informally provide support to one another. However, this interconnected yet dispersed network is not always sufficient for new scholars entering the field. This is an ever-growing market with increasing needs far surpassing what an informal support network can address or alleviate. More universities are offering graduate certificates in the field, ensuring the longevity of commitment from institutions to produce new scholars and scholarships in need of guidance in research and development.

We see this text as valuable to three primary groups: DH scholars interested in being in community with Black folks, either through collaborative partnerships or with texts that were created by, for, or about Black culture and experiences; Black Studies scholars who are beginning their journeys into DH and digital studies; and, funders, administrators, and stewards of Black DH projects. These three groups of people inevitably will and should work together on almost any internally or externally funded Black DH project. AADHum, for example, was the brainchild of Drs. Neil Fraistat and Sheri Parks. Dr. Fraistat served as the director of the Maryland Institute for Technology in the Humanities (MITH), and his research focused on DH, Romanticism, and textual studies. Dr. Parks served as Associate Dean for Research in the College of Arts and Humanities (ARHU) at the University of Maryland, and her research focused on Black cultural aesthetics, popular media, race, and gender. The project was supported by the Mellon Foundation and the University of Maryland's Dean of ARHU Bonnie Thornton Dill. Together, these scholars and separate entities imagined a Black DH initiative, bringing their different perspectives, experiences, and goals with them. Like any DH project, our initial funding and the subsequent team relied on differentiated knowledge as central to effective collaboration. So, however you come to Black DH, this text serves as an entry point to the community and conversation about doing this work with intention and care. Each chapter begins with key questions that provide a thematic preview of the chapter. Within the body of the text you will also find key lessons, fundamental principles, and guiding reflections.

For students at the start of their research, we suggest keeping a careful eye in this text on the places in your collaborative work where you can and must advocate for protections for yourself. Recognizing that this is not always an easy task, consider where you can find allies along the way. Choosing the right senior collaborators can provide you with care and support in your journey. Know that sometimes when you choose mentors and collaborators on principles of care, these folks may not have senior status in the field. Conversely, you may and will likely hold expertise in digital tools or research that your advisor or team leader may not. This is okay. Forging agreements early on will help you avoid and guard against others taking credit for your work. In this text, we advise you to think carefully about how the folks with whom you wish to work adhere to a radically intentional praxis of care in their supervision and advising. We also point you toward the second chapter of this text, "Where Are All the Black Scholars in DH?," as an orienting point to get more acquainted with the history of our field.

For those more advanced in their careers who are considering expanding or starting a Black DH project or center, we ask that you use this text to evaluate relationships with students and your responsibilities to them as collaborators and mentors. We want to pose the questions you should be asking yourself as you consider expanding your DH project or starting a new project. To that end, we encourage you to focus on the radical reflections at the end of each chapter as a mechanism of reflexivity about your own work. We also encourage you to think carefully about how to be intentional about crafting courses in Black DH, pointing you toward the fourth chapter of the text, and the kinds of programming that may best serve your community by reading the first chapter.

For potential community collaborators outside the academy, we encourage using this text to evaluate the utility of academic partnerships. Understanding the possibilities and limitations of working with both the academic and the layers of academic institutions is vital in assessing the appropriateness of sharing your intellectual labor. In our experience, community partnerships often fail during unspoken conversations over ownership of the work and academic institutions' capacities for providing resources. This text offers a behind-the-curtains look at the grant-making, negotiating, and programming process. We ask that community partners consider the value of joining established-center work versus partnering with academics to create new relationships—particularly with regards to the amount of financial or personnel resources required for the sustainability of your project.

As chairs, deans, and other university or institutional administrators, we hope this provokes you to better understand the needs and supports required by your faculty and student body in Black DH. We know Black DH projects are receiving more institutional funding than ever, and new faculty lines are being introduced (often at the junior level) to lead these centers and institutes. As leaders, it is incumbent upon you to protect the junior Black faculty that take up these positions. We hope you can gain more insight into what happens behind the scenes on Black DH projects from the narratives shared by the students and junior scholars in this text. The Black students, staff, and junior faculty responsible for everyday grant work are often over-burdened and under-supported. You can change this. We encourage you to use this text, especially the third chapter, to foster a more open and honest dialogue that allows care to rise in importance— *and* in policies and procedures—at your institutions. You can also use this text to begin the work of shifting existing policies around merit and promotion that encourage the kind of care and collaboration we advocate for in this book.

To our grant funding community, we invite you to read for sections that push for redefining the system's outreach and evaluation paradigms. How do we trouble the feedback loop between major research institutions and the grant funding bodies? Our experiences as grant funding recipients and grant application evaluators afford us a particular lens into how influential grant funders can be in making cultural shifts in the outputs of grant-funded projects. To be frank, what responsibility do grant funders have to evaluate the diversity and capacities of the suggested personnel? Agencies have to ask the questions, especially when the home institutions will not. Particularly, we solicit engagement with: the centrality of community outreach, existing procedures and practices for evaluating diversity in personnel and partnerships, and, accepted norms for establishing what is classified—or "what counts"—as Black or African American Studies projects. Is having African Americans as subjects sufficient in receiving funding for 19th and 20th century African American Studies projects? What does one's articulation of outreach say about how one values community and justice? How do we critically engage grant funders' power in making changes to the status quo of humanities projects?

How Did We Write It?

We were fortunate on our team to have expertise in oral history and qualitative fieldwork. From the project's earliest days, we knew we must be intentional about documenting our process. Any funded grant work must be accountable to funders and internal stakeholders. However, we also saw our accountability extending to our student/scholars community and the larger Black DH collective. AADHum's work was meant to touch those at the University of Maryland most directly, yet the vision of team members like Kevin Winstead led us to think about our place in helping guide a new network of scholars and scholarship that was intentionally digital and intentionally Black. Rather than positioning our research as a cure to the problems that ail Black DH, we instead see this work as a way to, as Dillard explains, begin to see our research as "a responsibility" (Dillard, 2016).

To serve as a conduit for new research and teaching models that center the lives and research of Black folks, we ensured that our mechanisms of record-keeping were firmly positioned in Black feminist epistemology. We first draw upon our former colleague Dr. Patricia Hill Collins' (2009) work in identifying four principles of Black feminist epistemology. These include (1) lived experience as a criterion of meaning, (2) the use of dialogue to assess knowledge claims, (3) the ethic of caring, and (4) the ethics of personal accountability.

In making a case for Black feminist study of Black folks, Kristal Moore Clemons cites Sophia Villenas (1996) to explain, "we are both the colonized and colonizer, marginalized by the academy yet using the resources and tools of the academy to write about our own communities and, even more intimately, our own lived experiences" (p. 713). We recognize the privilege we exercised at a research-intensive university with generous external funding. Further, we understand that even though many of us are Black scholars, being embedded within the university creates a distance from the Black communities we work with and write about. We, therefore set out, in our administration of DH programming and in our methodological approach for gathering our histories and preserving our data, to prioritize an Afrocentric methodological approach to data collection and preservation. Clemons (2019) describes the importance of an Afrocentric methodological approach. She explains that positionality, reciprocity, and reflexivity are critical to ethical work that is both by Black scholars and about Black communities. She outlines a roadmap for how to engage in transformative and intentional practices of care in our scholarship that work toward the goals of Black liberation, celebrate Black creativity and ingenuity, and simultaneously hold ourselves and those we study with accountable. From this directive, we base this book on practices of Black feminist autoethnography.

In her transformative text, *In the Wake*, Christina Sharpe describes her use of autobiography and autoethnography. She first cites Saidiya Hartman, writing,

> I include the personal here in order to position this work, and myself, in and of the wake. The 'autobiographical example … is not a personal story that folds onto itself; it's not about navel gazing, it's really about trying to look at historical and social process and one's own formation as a window onto social and historical processes, as an example of them.

Sharpe goes on, "Like Hartman, I include the personal here, 'to tell a story capable of engaging and countering the violence of abstraction'" (Sharpe, 2016, p. 8). We argue that using our own experiences forces us toward the goals of accountability, holds space for the importance of dialogue, promotes an ethic of caring, and requires our readers to witness lived experience as "a criterion of meaning."

What Should You Expect?

We have structured this book to draw upon our lived experiences, theory, and literature from Black studies, Black feminist thought, and DH. Rather than being prescriptive, we hope to use our successes and failings to trace a set of questions and guiding principles that may help scholars, funders, and administrators think more critically about their own work. This book occupies a unique space between research monographs and supplemental text. While our work is based on critical qualitative research, it also is written for an audience of practitioners (researchers, organizational unit heads, and graduate students) to prepare them to take on their own research and projects. Each chapter features guiding questions, bullet lists of practical advice, and radical reflections readers can use to implement best practices in their work. The book comprises five chapters, each engaging with a different component of doing Black DH. We begin with a formative question for readers: *What happens, in our conceptual approaches, programming, and teaching, when we center Black people?* Much of what remains so palpable to participants in AADHum's early years—liberation from expectations to manage white discomfort, disinvestment in intellectual posturing, safety to admit the confusion and uncertainty often admonished in graduate school, cross-generational connections that enabled collective care within academia's confines—owes itself to this call. Cultivating a new ethos of engagement and fostering genre-expanding connections may well be AADHum's most enduring legacy, and the most elusive to explain and describe.

In the first chapter, "I Don't Love DH; I Love Black Folks: Building Black DH Programming," we collectively explore the intricacies of attending to people and processes over products and deliverables. We reveal how intentional care is as much about what to disrupt and exclude—through a description of each of our core programs and initiatives—as it is about what to include and uplift. We draw heavily from our colleague Dr. Jovonne Bickerstaff's (2017) inspired work, "We who would build: Re-visioning resistance & theorizing beyond the gaze," to explore the considerations, missteps, and revelations that guided AADHum's early development and programming. We work to unveil the intensive emotional labor, all too often performed by Black women, required to cultivate dynamic initiatives and generative programming. We detail the multiple program initiatives of AADHum: Reading Groups, Conversation Series, Digital Humanities Incubators, AADHum Scholars, digitization efforts, and our national conference, *Intentionally Digital, Intentionally Black*. Just as AADHum offers lessons on how to serve as better stewards of Black wholeness—cultivating space for joy, weariness, hope, despair, abundance, mistakes, dreams, and more—it also suggests novel approaches institutions can take to support those charged with shepherding such initiatives into being.

In the next chapter, "Where Are All the Black Scholars in Black DH?: Creating Space for the Field of Black Digital Studies," Kevin C. Winstead traces the intellectual and administrative labor in the forging of a new field of study within Black Studies. Reading the formation of Black DH as a movement, Winstead delineates the intellectual community that led to a field that is informed by a politics of care, particularly by Black women scholars, to make new spaces for junior Black scholars to exist. In this chapter, we argue for a broader definition of Black DH that incorporates scholars who do not *make* or *build* traditional DH tools or products and instead focus on the study of Black gamers at play, Black writers on social media, and Black digital content creators. As we move through the work of our "forefamily" to the intentional care around institution building, Kevin concludes with thinking about how to sustain intellectual fellowship. We redefine Black DH from this perspective and provide practical guidance for how to take up this reinvigorated definition in building sustainable connections between those within and traditionally outside of DH research.

Our third chapter begins with a question: "What are we going to eat?" One thing the AADHum team consistently did was eat. But more importantly, we fed each other. In this chapter, Catherine Knight Steele considers what it means to be fed (both literally and figuratively) and how to move from DH collaborative work agreements to Black DH community through the care required to see colleagues and students in the fullness of their humanity. Here we turn to examples from the Black Panther Party's Free Breakfast Program and Psyche Williams-Forson's (2021) work, "Where Did They Eat? Where Did They Stay? Interpreting Material Culture of Black Women's Domesticity in the Context of the Colored Conventions," to consider how Black organizations—often through the invisible labor of Black women—intentionally attended to the physical, social and emotional needs of their community. Even as this work is ignored in the history of these racial projects in favor of the more visible parts of their programming, we recognize that we are better thinkers, writers, and teachers when our basic needs are met. Yet too often, the rapid production of DH projects silos people into roles on a research team and replicates the toxic culture of many aspects of hyper-capitalism. This chapter traces the linkages between caretaking through provision of actual food with the practice of crafting a community of research and teaching. Steele also outlines care as a method that attends to both historical work and social media analysis. We detail the decision-making process of forming equitable agreements for labor with student workers, creating a culture of rest, and rethinking provisions to support the work of Black DH.

Our fourth chapter, "If You Teach it, They Will Come: Developing Pedagogy for Black DH," written by Jessica H. Lu, examines the work of developing, practicing, and sustaining fundamental principles for Black DH teachers. Whether at the undergraduate or graduate levels, developing pedagogical ethics and practices in Black DH is essential to the overall development of the field and its future. This chapter therefore poses a guiding question: what is Black DH pedagogy? Drawing upon AADHum's efforts to introduce Black DH research and curricula to undergraduate students at the University of Maryland, we explore how Black feminist thought necessitates fundamental principles and practices for Black DH pedagogy, including: centering and affirming Black people as learners and teachers in the classroom; practicing care for students as whole persons; animating legacies of interdisciplinary power, resistance, and innovation in Black culture and community across the diaspora; and, moving beyond tools- or skills-focused instruction to engage theory-grounded critique of the impacts of emergent methods and technologies on the lives of Black people and their communities. When research, programming, and pedagogy align with radical intentionality, we can imagine and build Black DH classrooms that exist even in institutions lacking strong support for robust Black DH communities or programming.

The concluding chapter, "When and How to Walk Away," contains critical narrative reflections from each team member about how they came to work for AADHum and how they left that work. The end of the authors' service to the AADHum project brings the lesson of how, in the absence of intentionality, it is possible to retain funding but impossible to sustain a community. Collectively, as we process our own success, growth, and learning, we searched for concepts to help us understand the project's legacy as connected to the complicated histories of Black creatives, Black justice thinkers, and Black criticism, leading us to a Blues epistemology. Together, we offer a way of thinking of integrity-driven grant-funded projects through a lens of strategic assembly and disassembly in the face of changing opportunity structures and power relations.

Radical Intentionality argues that all Black DH programming must achieve three primary goals to be successful: first, the core of Black DH work must center the Black people doing the work and who will benefit from the work; second, Black DH must move beyond tools to engage in an intentional critique of the impact of technology on the lives of Black people; and, third, the future of Black DH is bound together in the intentional praxis of community building that breaks away from the siloed, individualistic and false meritocracy of the academy. Ultimately, we think there are many ways to achieve these goals, but it always begins with intentionality.

References

Bickerstaff, J. (2017). We who would build: Re-visioning resistance & theorizing beyond the gaze. African American History, Culture, and Digital Humanities (blog). February 18, 2017. https://web.archive.org/web/20211025065559/; https://aadhum.umd.edu/asante/2017/02/centralizing-blackness-digital-work/

Clemons, K. M. (2019, August 28). Black feminist thought and qualitative research in education. *Oxford Research Encyclopedia of Education.* https://doi.org/10.1093/acrefore/9780190264093.013.1194

Crompton, C., Lane, R. J., & Siemens, R. G. (Eds.). (2016). *Doing digital humanities: Practice, training, research.* Routledge.

Dillard, C. B. (2016). To address suffering that the majority can't see: Lessons from black women's leadership in the workplace. *New Directions for Adult and Continuing Education, 2016*(152), 29–38.

Hill Collins, P. (2009). *Black feminist thought: Knowledge, consciousness, and the politics of empowerment* (2nd ed.). Routledge. http://catdir.loc.gov/catdir/toc/ecip0827/2008037553.html

Hill Collins, P. (2013). *On intellectual activism.* Temple University Press. http://site.ebrary.com/id/10754191

hooks, bell (2006). *Outlaw culture: Resisting representations.* Routledge.

Risam, R. (2018). *New digital worlds: Postcolonial digital humanities in theory, praxis, and pedagogy.* Northwestern University Press.

Sharpe, C. E. (2016). *In the wake: On blackness and being.* Duke University Press.

Villenas, S. (1996). The colonizer/colonized Chicana ethnographer: Identity, marginalization, and co-optation in the field. *Harvard Educational Review, 66*(4), 711–732.

West, C. (April 17, 2011). *Justice is what love looks like in public.* Howard University. www.youtube.com/watch?v=nGqP7S_WO6o

Williams-Forson, P. (2021). Where did they eat? Where did they stay? Interpreting material culture of Black women's domesticity in the context of the Colored Conventions. In S. L. Patterson, P. G. Foreman, & J. Casey (Eds.), *The colored conventions movement: Black organizing in the nineteenth century.* UNC Press Books.

1

I DON'T LOVE DH; I LOVE BLACK FOLKS

Building Black DH Programming

Catherine Knight Steele, Jessica H. Lu, and Kevin C. Winstead

Every grant-funded project should probably have two proposals—one written for funders and one that is honest. Of course, no one sets out to write a dishonest proposal. Yet, all of us (including this book's authors, who have since submitted and been awarded private funding for other projects, labs, and centers) are beholden to the language and desires of internal and external funders, some of which contradict, impede, or delay the actual work we wish to accomplish. We are particularly cognizant of funding initiatives that force institutional partnerships forged out of a desire to leverage Black folks as currency in acquiring more funding. Projects that treat Black folks as a commodity do not typically lead to fruitful long-term relationships or programming that makes a difference. In this chapter, we use our experience with funded Black digital humanities (DH) projects to examine how, regardless of how programming may be funded or from whatever source it may emerge, it is possible to create a culture of radically intentional Black DH that centers Black people and Black culture.

The programming imperatives from the African American History, Culture, and Digital Humanities Initiative (AADHum) proposal were born out of a desire to showcase the University of Maryland's existing strengths. While none of us was a part of the team that wrote the initial grant proposal, it quickly became our task to interpret and implement its mandates. The primary work of AADHum was to "work with digital and archival repositories of primary source materials that privilege understanding of African American experiences; and disseminate knowledge gained at the intersections of DH and African American labor, migration, and artistic expression" ("Synergies among Digital Humanities and African American History and Culture: An Integrated Research and Training Model," 2015) through the implementation of an incubator program run by the Maryland Institute of Technology in the Humanities (MITH) and curricular development

DOI: 10.4324/9781003299134-2

through the existing First-Year Intensive Research Experience (FIRE) program. We were to establish "programming that will bring together research and technical experts with a broader public and will increase the accessibility and impact of both the project themes and methods of analysis" ("Synergies among Digital Humanities and African American History and Culture: An Integrated Research and Training Model," 2015). These were reasonable, well-articulated goals. Yet they, like many project's narratives, were written to celebrate our institution's existing university faculty and centers. Because institutions with already existing funds and resources can more readily demonstrate their capacity to do more with even more money, they (we) are who usually benefit most from DH funding. *This* is the proposal you write for funders—the proposal that focuses on your strengths and ignores the actual reasons why you need a grant on your campus. Why would an institution like ours need the resources and staffing that a grant like this could provide? Primarily because major institutions often function in silos, with labor shortages, and without the resources for faculty to spend time training and mentoring inside and outside the classroom on projects that may not yield a publication or path to tenure.

The honest proposal is reflexive, fluid, and open to challenge and critique from those the work hopes to touch. Unlike the proposal that secures funding, the honest proposal recognizes and reflects on why this work and these partnerships have not already been formed with all the institutional strengths you may already have. In developing the programming for AADHum, we actively sought out departments, programs, and external partners with whom we could forge or repair relationships and create programs that centered Blackness. In this chapter, we outline the serious moves this team made in interpreting and reconceiving the original asks of the Synergies among Digital Humanities and African American History and Culture grant proposal and, in doing so, birthing the AADHum Initiative.

The worlds in which Synergies was conceived and AADHum was realized were, in some ways, in stark contrast. Funding for AADHum came in early 2016, yet the programming for the grant started early in 2017. As AADHum Postdoctoral Associate Dr. Justin Hosbey wrote in January of that year,

> Here we stand, weeks removed from the inauguration of the 45th president of the United States … Now we must ask—where do we go from here? As scholars and intellectuals committed to critical Black study and Black studies, where do our responsibilities and accountabilities lie?
>
> *(Hosbey, 2017)*

In revisiting Justin's words, we reflected on what it was like to return to campus after the inauguration. We witnessed colleagues in tears, unable to wrap their minds around what this new political climate would mean for their jobs in the humanities, their rights, and their bodily autonomy. We were not immune to their fear or trepidation but also did not carry the privilege of being shocked or left unable to move forward. We were instead ready to battle and build. As then Post doctoral Associate Jovonne Bickerstaff wrote,

> My hope in the AADHum initiative is that we move towards what Brittney Cooper calls "liberatory world-making"—imagining new ways of seeing and thinking about that intersection of digital studies and African American research. We battle, and we build … and we choose the work to which we'll devote our hands each day.
>
> *(Bickerstaff, 2017)*

We originally conceptualized this chapter with Jovonne Bickerstaff, who served as a Postdoctoral Associate for AADHum. Jovonne interviewed for the position with the same forthright honesty she brought each day to the office. She let us know up front that she is not a DHer. She did not make or code anything and had no interest in learning how to do so for this project. Because of her previous work with the David C. Driskell Center, she had experience collecting oral narratives and digitizing them for her and others' research. But—as she always makes clear—her research is about love, gender, race, family, and emotions. Her hire was an intentional effort to bring a non-DH voice to a prominent position of AADHum leadership. In her interview, we heard about how her dissertation, entitled "Together, Close, Resilient: Essays on Emotion Work Among Black Couples," examines African American couples in enduring relationships (10–40 years) in Cleveland, New York, and Chicago. She examined couples' strategies and perspectives on emotional carework—the neglected dimension of family work. Theorizing from Black couples' experience, her work disturbed the trend of taking educated, white, middle-class couples as the normative American family and reveals how our conceptualization of emotion work might benefit from greater consideration of social positionality. In other words, she is invested in what happens when Black folks are the center or norm rather than at the margins of how we understand what it means to love and provide care.

More than anything else, Jovonne constantly reminded us that she didn't love Black DH—she loved Black folks—and that if our project was to be of any value to Black people, it must keep that fundamental truth at the core. While Jovonne was not able to join us in writing this project,[1] we still see her hire, her insight, and her labor as integral to how we designed and implemented the AADHum initiative. She is, therefore, an architect of how we approach this chapter. In each of the following sections, we walk you through one arm of our initiative's programming. We do so with the hopes of pulling back the curtain on how we worked as a team to develop new programs and match them to the needs and interests of our community of scholars. In describing AADHum's programming, we hope to meet one of the primary aims of the grant: developing replicable models for Black DH that can function in varied environments, with varied resources. Interspersed in each section are quotes from Bickerstaff's (2017) essay, "We who would build: Re-visioning resistance & theorizing beyond the gaze," written for the AADHum website in early 2017.[2] We use her words in this chapter as we did during her three-year term with the grant, as a north star and guidepost.

In that essay Dr. Bickerstaff wrote the following,

> Recently, activist Brittany Packnett developed a Twitter thread which be-gan, "We have two hands: one is to battle, one is to build." Certainly, we African Americanists know how to battle. So much of our training as scholars prepares us for it; we're socialized to privilege the work of critique and deconstruction …Taking Packnett's call for a multifaceted strategy of resistance to heart, I must ask, when do we build?

This chapter answers the questions not only of when we build but how. We ask the reader to consider what is required to disrupt the leveraging of Black folks as currency in DH grants and, instead, reposition Black people at the center of the work.

KEY QUESTIONS

- What can we do to ensure Black folks, rather than DH tools, are at the center of our work?
- How can planning and programming in Black DH move beyond sites of struggle and resistance toward work that centers liberation and love?
- How do we balance our obligations to our funders and stakeholders with our obligations to the Black communities we hope to serve with our work?

Developing Programming for Black Folks and DH

Reading Groups and Conversation Series

In spring 2017, AADHum launched a robust slate of public programming, begin-ning with a semester-long series of Reading Groups—six in total—that invited participants to engage with a selection of scholarly texts. Thematically organized for each Reading Group, the texts animated key questions and debates across different fields and disciplines with relevant connections to Black DH. In some instances, a featured scholar was invited to help guide the conversation; in others, the Reading Group convened in a special location that brought AADHum into community with others.

As we imagined the Reading Groups, we were faced with a tremendous opportunity to introduce AADHum's burgeoning community to our approach to and vision for Black DH. We took this chance—and challenge—seriously;

we knew many participants would be relatively new to Black Studies, DH, or both. Those who attended the Reading Groups were both junior and established scholars, often well-versed in foundational concepts, varying modes of inquiry, and the practices of scholarly research and reading in their own respective disciplines. Our charge was to curate readings that would bring us together in intellectual kinship. We aimed not for completeness but for connection between seemingly disparate fields of inquiry and methods—connections that would inspire new ways of thinking and doing in Black digital research and study.

We considered—and swiftly rejected—two initial temptations: first, to structure the Reading Groups in terms that charted the emergence, development, and future of DH; and second, to frame DH wholly in terms of the marginalization of Blackness and Black folks in the field. Both approaches would have grounded AADHum in a deficit model of thinking. As Jovonne recognized from the outset, such a confrontational framing is common "given how Black folk have been conceptualized or written out of canons[…] But … is that enough?" We determined that the Reading Groups could be a space in which the fullness of Black life and culture could take center stage in ways that would challenge us to do the work of "theorizing beyond gaze," as Jovonne calls it, and "imagine new narratives and inquiry" for DH that did not begin and end with identifying and lamenting the exclusion of Black people from the field.

Our first guidepost was a commitment to defining for ourselves how Black DH can "name, frame, and lay claim to different terrains." It was imperative to us to chart the scope of Black DH conversations to center and extend welcome to folks that did not already see themselves as part of existing DH networks and literatures. Our primary strategy was to identify and articulate Reading Group themes focused on Black people, rather than on popular tools or concepts in DH, such as:

- *Holding Space*: providing participants with a critical foundation for understanding the language, concepts, and frameworks that guide some of the most pressing questions and dilemmas in Black digital scholarship
- *Where and When We Enter*: examining the empirical and ethical considerations that inform the strengths, pitfalls, and potential of varied theoretical approaches for exploring the African American experience
- *Geographies and Genealogies of Knowledge*: surveying the historical and contemporary landscape of Black digital research, tracing its development and evolution
- *Theorizing "the Archive"*: exploring one of the fundamental tools of Black digital scholarship—the archive—and examining how the authority, reliability, and completeness of the archive can be challenged when scholars engage with resources in traditional, unorthodox, and unanticipated ways
- *Intersectionality and Critical Race Theory*: situating Black digital scholarship within two of the most prominent frameworks for understanding African American history and culture, in conversation with pioneers in these fields, Dean Bonnie Thornton Dill and Dr. Patricia Hill Collins

- *A Room of Our Own: Trials and Triumphs of Generating Theory*: reflecting on how scholars can use their newly acquired conceptual and empirical approaches to cultivate and refine their theoretical sensibilities and empirical orientations to digital Blackness

These themes guided us toward scholarship by Black people, about Black people, as the primary entry point to discussing, interrogating, and understanding the complexities of digital affordances and technologies in humanities research. Rather than beginning with the confines and constraints of existing DH literature and attempting to insert Black perspectives, AADHum started with the notion that Black thinkers, Black history, and Black culture could and should inform how we think about and practice DH. We drew from writings in Black Studies, information science, African American Studies, sociology, communication, history, American Studies, media studies, gender and queer studies, and more to craft reading lists and materials that placed Black people at the center of each conversation and recognized their integral roles in shaping, challenging, and innovating our digital worlds.

The Reading Groups, therefore, challenged us to position ourselves within and among ever-shifting communities of thought—communities with varying levels of attachment to DH scholarship and practices. With each session, we aimed to inspire our participants to digest, interrogate, and intervene together in conversations without seeking to end them. We were fortunate to host scholars whose books and articles we read—such as André Brock, who joined us as he worked on *Distributed Blackness: African American Cybercultures* (2020). Rather than asking Brock to give a talk on the work, or to teach us about his research, we aimed instead for a discursive space where folks could ask questions, make intercessions, and push him to think about his work—and our participants' work—differently. We wanted AADHum's community to approach the Reading Groups as a starting point for thinking beyond their disciplinary instincts and allegiances and imagining, instead, novel ways of pursuing the questions that shape their research, teaching, and lives. In those early days, the Reading Groups established a fundamental imperative of AADHum's work, responsive to Kyla Wazana Tompkins's (2012) reminder: "we aren't here to learn what we already know."

The Reading Groups explored how non-DH perspectives could broaden the field in ways that centered Black people, rather than tacking them on as an addendum or correction to existing work. AADHum's Reading Groups also demonstrated how intentionally interdisciplinary thinking prompted boundary-crossing conversations that might not otherwise thrive within tool-centered DH theories and practices. As AADHum's fledgling community of DH-curious scholars and researchers began to take seriously their own potential contributions to DH, we saw that the Reading Groups series needed to grow.

By fall 2017, the Reading Groups evolved into a different sort of exercise: a Conversation Series comprising six public dialogues, each of which featured a panel of carefully selected scholars, practitioners, and community members with expertise related to particular themes. For instance, the first installment, entitled "Libraries: Justice, Technology, and Culture," assembled Tahira Akbar-Williams, an Education and African American Studies Librarian at the University of Maryland; Dr. Nicole Cooke, then an Assistant Professor at the School of Information Sciences at the University of Illinois at Urbana-Champaign; Dr. Howard Dodson, former Director of the Moorland-Spingarn Research Center and Howard University Libraries, and formerly the long-time director of the Schomburg Center for Research in Black Culture; and Trevor Muñoz, then–Interim Director of the Maryland Institute for Technology in the Humanities and Assistant Dean for Digital Humanities Research at the University of Maryland Libraries.

Where the Reading Groups relied on intense study and discussion of already-published works, the Conversation Series prioritized active and impromptu dialogue. Beyond the logistics of arranging for speakers to travel to campus, the organization was simple: we honed in on topics, issues, or spaces that our community seemed most invested in. Then, we looked for folks who could bring relevant experiences to bear upon an engaging, productive dialogue. While seemingly simple in design, the Conversation Series was an intentional effort to put a group of people in one room and allow them to teach, learn, and question together. Each speaker arrived at the event without prior knowledge of what questions may be asked of them, and the audience, too, was not prompted to prepare in any way. Each session of the Conversation Series was convened simply by its title, a hint at what the speakers may share in common or where their work might connect or diverge. We delegated the task of moderating and shaping each conversation to Jovonne, whose expertise in oral history, qualitative research, and interviewing equipped her with a rare gift that speaks to a foundational truth of teaching and community-building: "there is a conversation in the room that only these people at this moment can have. Find it" (Brown, 2017, p. 41).[3]

Taken together, both the Reading Groups and Conversation Series set a tone for our intentional efforts to lead with love for Black people and Black communities first. We were driven by both the desire and necessity to share knowledge from existing literatures about Black history and culture as a precursor to exploring DH, as well as to platform Black scholars and those who work with Black artifacts and texts as teachers and experts in their respective fields. We began AADHum's work with an honest accounting of what our community knew, what they hoped to learn, and what they could offer one another. These dialogues, therefore, offered us more of a blueprint for moving forward than the original grant proposal ever could.

Digital Humanities Incubators

Among AADHum's public programming, Digital Humanities Incubators (DHI) were among the few offerings that were explicitly required by the original grant proposal, which proposed "a series of workshops, tutorials, 'office hours,' and project consultations that organize the high-level training intended to acculturate scholars, students, and librarians to the use of digital humanities tools and method" ("Synergies among Digital Humanities and African American History and Culture: An Integrated Research and Training Model," 2015). These workshops were originally conceived in traditional DH terms, as methods-focused spaces that would "provide a progressive arc of skill development relevant to digital work [with] testbed collections, encompassing transcription and/or digitization principles, data modeling, metadata, and basic data exploration" ("Synergies among Digital Humanities and African American History and Culture: An Integrated Research and Training Model," 2015). According to the original grant proposal, the incubators would be characterized by project "pitches," "targeted readings on methodologies," "homework assignments," and "one-on-one meetings and coaching" for projects limited to questions of "labor, migration and/or artistic expression."

The constraints of such a traditional DH workshop model were immediately clear. Not only was there little mention or explanation of how the incubators would be tailored to meaningfully serve Black communities, in particular, but the emphasis on skills acquisition also suited neither the realities of AADHum's growing audience nor our human-centered approach to doing Black DH. In even the earliest months, we realized that the community hungry for AADHum's support and resources needed more than a refresher course in the latest tools and technologies; instead, they needed genuine, attentive, and sustained support to investigate, play, and create with digital methods. AADHum workshops therefore needed to be reconceived as spaces for exploration and experimentation rather than structured assembly lines for digital projects. So, in spring 2017, we invited people to come in curious, launching a DHI series that became the most popular and prominent fixture in AADHum's programming.

The spring 2017 DHI series comprised four workshops meant to foster questions related to race, place, and space in Black DH: Surveying the Terrain, Meaning and Mapping, Time and Narrative, and Representing Movement. The following year, we extended the series by focusing specifically on notions of movement in historical, contemporary, and future Black life. In four distinct installments, AADHum's DHI series continued with: Movement of Ideas, Movement of the Body & the Black Arts Movement, Movement of People, and Social Movements.

Taken together, we reconceived of DHI workshops as sites of curiosity and exploration that presumes that Black DH work begins with Black people—rather than the tools or technologies that can facilitate research. Each session provided resources to equip curious graduate students and faculty, of varying levels of experience, with digital tools to better tackle humanistic inquiry. Participants learned the standards and practices of the Text Encoding Initiative (TEI) markup language; how to identify and organize data relationships using databases; fundamental principles and platforms for mapping geospatial data; how network maps can be used to visualize connections; novel methods for collecting large-scale datasets from social media discourse; and more. But we took great care to frame skills acquisition as a resource—not the goal—of Black DH, so investigations of Black life always preceded and grounded our exploration of digital tools.

AADHum's goal in conceiving and facilitating the DHI workshops were to move participants beyond skills or tools acquisition and toward richer engagement with the roles of technology in Black people's lives. As such, each DHI session demanded intensive preparation from our staff. We were acutely aware that it would have been much easier to structure and plan a workshop based purely on technical training. For instance, digital methods of collecting, organizing, analyzing, and publishing data for research are common in fields such as information science and computer science; as such, numerous online tutorials and demonstrations could have supported participants to pursue these skills independently. That sort of learning may have produced new DH researchers, but in our view, it could never support Black DH scholars. So we undertook efforts to devise new models of training that would meaningfully ground technical skills training in rich historical and cultural contexts.

Yet, radical intentionality does not mean we planned every moment and intervention from the outset. On one occasion, our team sat together to work on our mastery of Airtable, a popular platform for building databases, workflows, and project management systems. We decided to pursue this goal by approaching lyrics data from the Genius website to think through space, place, and hip hop. Members of our team had experienced formative parts of their lives in different areas fundamentally shaped by Black music cultures, such as Chicago, Philadelphia, and Atlanta. This sparked an initial interest in how Black sonics and Black spaces connect. How did artists talk about geographies? When did they use geographically specific language in their lyrics, and where instead did they insert culturally specific, yet geographically ambiguous terms like "the corner"? As we played in a space we intentionally crafted to be safe for curiosity and inquisitiveness—where we gave folks the freedom to fail, and where the value of exploring Black culture for its own sake did not have to be justified to a skeptical audience—something rather unexpected, yet amazing, happened. Instead of tracking the rhetoric of space and place, we ended up tracking the movement of sound, inadvertently identifying the producers and the geographic spaces that birthed trap music and how the music spread across the American South to the rest of the country. With the gathered data from Genius, we built a network map (see Figure 1.1) that told not only the story of Atlanta producers and their studies, but also of how we learned the importance of centering our work on Black culture and letting the tools guide us where they may. This was not our original intention, but it started to shape how we prepared for following DHI sessions.

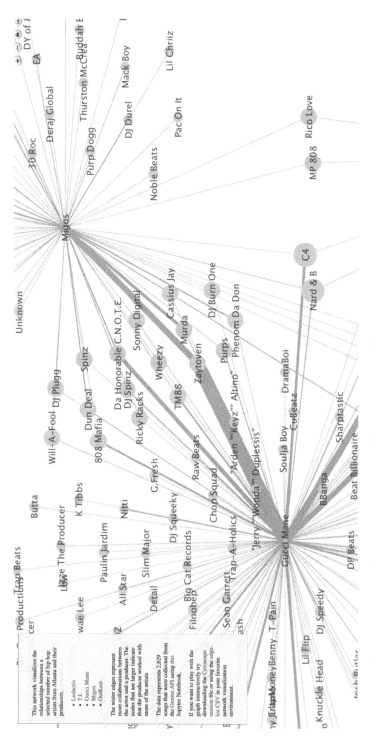

FIGURE 1.1 A partial capture of a network map created by AADHum staff and Ed Summers, former developer at Maryland Institute for Technology in the Humanities (MITH).

A similar process was repeated for each DHI. In hours of meetings preceding each workshop, we meticulously drafted written tutorials, handouts, and exemplar materials; outlined key points and questions for discussion; envisioned the interplay of dialogue, demonstration, and hands-on play; connected skills to critical theory and scholarship; and identified community members with relevant expertise or experience to contribute to the conversation. In undertaking this work, we aimed to cultivate digital skill-building that remains conscious and careful of how Black people's lives, histories, and cultures are intertwined with technology.

Like our other programs, the DHIs were reimagined as human-centered, Black-centered sites of care and nuance. It would have been easier to employ a more traditional DH model of skills instruction, to limit our conversations about tools in terms of how each could either help or harm Black scholarship, or to discuss Black digital technologies as offshoots of or responses to mainstream digital practice. Instead, we challenged ourselves and our participants to wrestle with how DH might offer intellectual and practical mechanisms for both battling and building. Echoing Brittany Packnett's words, Jovonne continually prompted us to remember:

> We have two hands: one is to battle, one is to build. We battle. We resist by calling out threats to our dignity by name. We build. We actively protect our dignity by creating what works. Those two hands may be on one person, one organization may be set up to do both. For others, they are the battling or the building kind. Either way, the battlers need the builders. The builders need the battlers. This is a discipline of resistance.
>
> *(Bickerstaff, 2017)*

We sought to shape and support AADHum—and, with it, Black DH—as a community welcoming to both battlers and builders, with the resources for both to engage with, learn from, and grow among one another.

In our efforts to do so, we hoped to foster empowerment among participants to choose for themselves how Black DH may serve or supplement their work. In Jovonne's words,

> Ultimately, how, when and why we enter as African Americanists, seems to turn largely on who we are working for and what we are working towards. The aim is not to abandon the battle, but simply to recognize that, while necessary, it is insufficient. [Our] hope in the AADHum initiative is that we move towards what Brittney Cooper calls 'liberatory world-making'— imagining new ways of seeing and thinking about that intersection of digital studies and African American research. We battle and we build … and we choose the work to which we'll devote our hands each day.
>
> *(Bickerstaff, 2017)*

AADHum Scholars

As cornerstones of AADHum's programming, the Reading Groups, Conversation Series, and DHIs helped us to convene a burgeoning community of people— humanities researchers, DHers, community partners and activists, and artists— who were interested in work at the intersections of Black life and the digital. The community was diverse and varied in levels of experience, technical knowledge, and intellectual and practical goals. For well over a year and a half, rotating locations and topics, these sessions allowed AADHum participants to deepen their skills and gave our staff a chance to listen to what the community needed most.

It became clear that one thing they needed was something that the original grant proposal never envisioned, and ultimately was relatively easy for us to pass on to them: a formalized *association* with the AADHum grant itself, with the Maryland Institute for Technology in the Humanities and with the Andrew W. Mellon Foundation. As many folks in graduate school, in faculty positions, and in contingent/contract roles already know, much of the work we do as scholars, researchers, and teachers—including the time we spend seeking productive communities and training new skills—is not recognized by the academy in ways that are visible, let alone legible, outside of our home departments or institutions.

We were primarily inspired by the many graduate students that had found refuge, motivation, and support in AADHum's community. They were tackling their dissertations, with many approaching the finish line and looking ahead toward positions both within and beyond the academy. We knew these graduate students would need more than a robust skillset and sharp critical insights in order to thrive; they needed a way to declare or quantify exactly what they had been doing with us for the past two years. It is a common refrain that hints at the layers of (in)visibility that comprise academic labor: *they needed something to put on their CV.*

With this imperative, the idea for AADHum Scholars was born. It was a chance for us to leverage the resources of the grant and distill some of the most productive elements of our cornerstone programming in service of a small cohort of learners. What might happen if they could spend a year thinking and learning together? Could we provide a vocabulary and structure for those outside the AADHum community and our institution to recognize their sustained investment in Black DH research and training, and the expertise they had gained? Could we focus some of what we had learned from building a large-scale Black DH initiative to care especially for a smaller group of people, each facing their own unique needs, goals, and challenges?

AADHum Scholars was launched in fall 2017 as an effort to showcase, support, and celebrate the work of six researchers striving to make an impact at the crossroads of Black history, Black culture, and the digital. Each Scholar was asked to present their work to the broader AADHum community in a workshop setting; to guest-author a blog post published on AADHum's website; and, to attend a series of one-on-one mentoring and skills-development sessions with members of both AADHum and MITH staff. In exchange, AADHum provided Scholars with a venue and community for soliciting and receiving feedback about their research-in-progress; individualized attention to help them think through technical and conceptual obstacles in their work; and direct material support in the form of summer research grants and seed funding to jumpstart their Black DH projects.

Drawn from different disciplines, career stages, and regional institutions, the first cohort included: Hazim Abdullah-Smith (American Studies, UMD), Dr. Richard Bell (History, UMD), Dr. Brandi Brimmer (History & Geography, Morgan State University), Alyson Farzad-Phillips (Communication, UMD), Leticia Ridley (Theater & Performance Studies, UMD), and Dr. Tyechia Thompson (English, Howard University). The following 2018–2019 year, we extended the AADHum Scholars program to welcome: Kimberly Bain (English & Interdisciplinary Humanistic Study, Princeton University), Yvonne Bramble (American Studies, UMD), Dr. Imani Cheers (Global Media Project), Jordan Ealey (Theater & Performance Studies, UMD), Stan Maxson (History, UMD), and Dr. Rhondda Robinson Thomas (English, Clemson University).

In carefully reviewing applications to ultimately select the members of each AADHum Scholars cohort, we intentionally focused on early career scholars—namely, assistant professors or junior faculty; non-tenure-track faculty, especially at historically Black colleges and universities; and graduate students. We believed these groups were poised to benefit most productively from an infusion of funding, collegial feedback, and skills training to help them move from ideation to experimentation and, ultimately, meaningful execution. The AADHum Scholars selected were ready to learn new skills and analyze the historical, cultural, and social impacts of digital tools, but most had not yet begun to imagine fully fleshed-out Black DH projects. While the DHIs introduced them to new possibilities and important questions for consideration, the 90-minute sessions seemed to always cut learning short. They needed more, and we had the opportunity to give. From the beginning, AADHum Scholars was not conceived as a mechanism for funding projects; with each Scholar selected, we were funding a person.

This approach was an intentional departure from traditional DH funding in two ways. First, traditional DH funding often seeks fully conceptualized projects with a leader who already has the skillsets to make it happen. We believe instead that Black DH may chart a different—arguably radical—path: to see the potential in an individual's scholarship and provide them the space, resources, and funds necessary to think through their ideas; and to provide them with support and community to help them learn the skills they need to move forward with implementation of their project. We further conceptualized AADHum Scholars to disrupt the strict boundaries of existing DH funding structures, especially with regard to time. We neither demanded nor expected AADHum Scholars to complete a proposed project during the term of the grant period and were therefore less concerned about the immediate results of their work within an academic term. Instead, we made it a priority for AADHum Scholars to access the spaces and communities they needed to grow into their scholarship—even if that prompted more questions than answers or revealed more potential pathways than complete deliverables. We sought out folks who were genuinely committed to Black Studies, and invested most enthusiastically in scholars whose tepid interests in DH or the digital could be cultivated with time, grace, and patience.

Second, traditional DH funding often seeks out prominent or already-established scholars that can bring visibility and validity to a program, which often makes them more valuable to an institution. Having navigated the grant proposal and administration process for three years, it has been our observation that the appearance of prestige, and the mutually beneficial attachment of big names to even bigger institutions, is a valuable currency. This approach reveals much about the current state of the academy and the ways it allocates resources and accolades. However, funding already very well-funded scholars from private institutions, funding senior scholars who have previously received ample grant support, or funding prominent scholars who can leverage their already-established reputations in order to access privileged spaces and opportunities does little to actually enrich the field with new skills, innovative methods, or fresh thinkers. For Black DH, an alternative approach—one that actively seeks to make space for scholars, researchers, and teachers whose potential has not yet been recognized or materially supported—may serve to benefit the growth and development of the entire community while disrupting the corrupted systems that too often organize the distribution of funding at our institutions.

The creation of AADHum Scholars exemplified some of the other vital lessons we had learned from two years of programming. For instance, we had seen firsthand that groups of students and faculty working on different projects could be of service to one another; through collaboration across disciplines and existing methodological commitments, a Black DH community could thrive and grow. It was further undeniable that the provision of material resources (time, skills training, and monetary compensation) are essential to the support of scholars and teachers. Any effort to build and sustain a scholarly community without these reinforcements runs the risk of demanding more of its participants rather than providing refuge and relief. Finally, we can and must do what we can to recognize the labor that Black DH work requires of its pioneers and stewards. With the distinction of AADHum Scholars, our cohorts would signal to future employers or tenure review boards that they had not only undertaken sustained efforts to grow their own skillsets and advance their careers but that they had also contributed meaningfully to the growth of Black DH as a field.

While the AADHum Scholars program was never part of the original grant, its operation became a pillar and priority of our Black DH praxis. AADHum Scholars continually reminded us to trust folks to tell us what they need, and never to develop programming without community input. In casual exchanges about departments lacking accessible advisors in the opening moments of a Reading Group, or an offhand remark about dissertation stress during a DHI, our community showed us that they needed things a grant proposal could hardly articulate or capture. Some of them were part of AADHum because they needed to learn how to use a new tool; others kept coming back because they needed to feel involved in the act of crafting or building something new. Almost everyone, though, had practical, urgent needs that invaded every aspect of their academic and professional lives. They needed to finish graduate school, they needed to find and secure jobs, and they needed funding in order to be able to eat. As we'll discuss in a later chapter, this idea of care and feeding bled into every component of what we did with AADHum. With AADHum Scholars, we had found a new way to care for the community—to feed their minds as well as their bellies—and share the resources we had.

Digital Archives

The AADHum project offered various programs and initiatives catered to the students and larger Black digital studies communities in and around the University of Maryland. But at its start, as many DH projects do, it focused on digitizing historical records. The grant writers astutely wrote the project proposal to emphasize the strengths of our campus. As the initial news release for AADHum noted:

> The essential tensions between labor, migration and artistic expression in the development of African American diasporic cultures in the United States form the rich core of the Synergies project. These themes represent some of the College of Arts and Humanities (the College) greatest strengths and will bring together prominent and nationally-recognized faculty in African American history and cultural studies from departments throughout the University of Maryland.
>
> (Maryland Center for Humanities Research, 2016)

One of those strengths was the extensive archival records housed on our campus, including the George Meany Memorial AFL-CIO Archive, which was the largest single donation to the university libraries ever. The archive was valued at $25 million and "contained more than 40 million artifacts and documents ranging from campaign buttons and photographs to books and even a pair of old work boots" (Hottle, 2013). Synergies among Digital Humanities and African American History and Culture were less concerned with the work boots and more with records of how the AFL-CIO's fights for worker's rights intersected with the civil rights movement. Specifically, these digitized records, along with those from the David Driskell Center, would serve as a "testbed." The records from these separate entities were grouped in the proposal but required entirely different digitization procedures and separately taught us valuable lessons about digitizing in Black DH.

The George Meany Memorial AFL-CIO Archive was under the care of University of Maryland's special collections archivists, who already had procedures in place for digitization. Our grant provided funding and the work of identifying parts of the collections relevant to African American history. Our desires, timeline, and process were often out of step with the plans that already existed in Special Collections. The Driskell Center's collections were stored and maintained within a different system, and identifying important records required more workers and more time than allotted in our proposal. We were asking the center to do work they didn't have workers to support during a time when they frankly had more important things to do.

Digitizing historical records around slavery and the racial justice movement is a frequent request for major funding agencies. AADHum was no exception. Having been given this goal rather than it emerging from our knowledge and experience with the community of scholars engaged with AADHum, we were left to wonder,

> Might our preoccupation with Black struggle, whether in the conditions of or resistance to oppression, make us complicit in the diminishing the fullness of black humanity and what we might explore in it? Can we imagine examining black experience without making America's racialization project the dominant idiom?
>
> *(Bickerstaff, 2017)*

We struggled as the project advanced to see how this part of the proposal aligned with what the grant had evolved to become. As we increasingly shifted away from "making" and digitizing toward conversations among cohorts, we wondered if it were possible to make this digitization project work for the scholars and community we were building. To engage with these digitized records as "testbeds," we needed to determine what exactly we were to test—their use in research projects? Classroom assignments? Something else? Our primary concern was not to allow the digitization project to overtake the varied and exceedingly more exciting ideas emerging from students and our greater community about what a Black DH initiative could do to change the campus and field. Rather than force a fit, we asked our graduate assistants to consider how they might use the records in their work, whether that be a dissertation, course, or DH project.

We chose intentionality. Kevin and Jessica started as graduate assistants on the project, devoting 20 hours per week to AADHum. But, we were also fortunate enough to have two additional graduate assistants for much of the three-year initiative. The first was Melissa Brown, a sociologist and scholar of Black feminist thought, digital sociology, social movements, and sexual politics. The second was

Will Thomas, an information studies scholar focusing on formalized information organization and the document systems which organized slavery-based industrial production. Both were integral members of the team, and their curiosity and creativity provided us with a mechanism to bring these digitized records to communities on campus who would not typically see them or even know of their existence.

Melissa Brown looked critically at how Black women were excluded from the AFL-CIO labor archives. She scoured the crevices and cracks to pull out the words and images of Black women like Coretta Scott King, who is often only discussed in the shadows of her husband's legacy. The now *Dr.* Brown demonstrated how these digitized records provided increased accessibility while reinforcing the exclusion of Black women. She led a digital storytelling session, teaching participants how to use ArcGIS StoryMaps while holding space for the reality that telling Black women's stories is sometimes made more, not less difficult, when digitization efforts reinforce misogynoir. Sometimes, when scholars access more records, the likelihood of assuming the records hold the full and complete picture increases. In these cases, the digitization only serves to codify the exclusion of Black women and queer folks who were intentionally overlooked in many records from racial justice movements. Dr. Brown's StoryMap made this point clear. But, even more importantly, her session ensured that the students and faculty first encountering these archives through their work with AADHum could not ignore this reality in their own work going forward.

Melissa's work with the digitized material resulted in interest from behavioral and social sciences scholars and historians in the humanities, while Will spent more time on the process, often scouring existing research guides, pulling documents from boxes, and selecting materials. Will's informatics background and a keen interest in labor made this a good fit. He established a research unit in our incubator series on mapping and migration (see Figure 1.2), re-focusing our attention on the space we held at the university and forcing many of us to learn and reconcile with the past and present of Black folks living in Prince George's County, Maryland.

This session walked participants, in four parts, through the process of building and generating maps in QGIS (a free and open source geographic information system), but only by thinking carefully about the migratory decisions of Black families in Prince George's county over multiple decades. Will asked us to consider how archival materials can capture only a portion of a spatial project (see Figure 1.3). His work in digitizing the records challenged us to think more carefully about what comes of the records. When Black folks create and leave behind, who acquires them, and how do they get used?[4]

Part of our trepidation about the digitization portion of our initiative's imperatives is that it is the only set of circumstances where we had to qualify our work. To pull pieces of records for digitization, we had to explicitly name some portion as being about "Black labor," "Black migration," or "Black artistic expression," when, as Jovonne Bickerstaff reminds us,

When the university was founded, the Prince George's County Jail held people running away from slavery. By 2001, Nelson Mandela would give the Sadat Lecture on campus, and be made an honorary Marylander by Parris Glendening, then Governor -- and former County Executive.

In this module, we'll take the theme *Reflection and Self-Reflection: Prince George's County 1974 - 1994*, and ask new questions of our maps with tools like Qgis and PostGIS. We'll ask questions of spaces and places and narrative to see how this corner of the world changed in people's eyes. Through this lens, we will try to glimpse the complexity of Black migration from within.

In 1974, Prince George's County, Maryland was seen as a white jurisdiction, especially in contrast to its neighbor, the District of Columbia. By 1994, Prince George's County was seen as a Black jurisdiction. But the change was more than how the county looked on the outside. The self-perception of the county changed; people looked at themselves differently both individually and collectively. In this module, we'll take the theme *Reflection and Self-Reflection: Prince George's County 1974 - 1994*, to complicate questions of migration. We ask new questions of our maps with open-source tools like QGIS (Geographic Information System) and PostGIS (backend GIS database)-- drawing digital maps showing places (church buildings, street corners) intersecting with spaces (census tracts, electoral districts) characterized by narratives (newspaper article sentiments). What are the cultural markers and what is the cultural narrative of the migration of people in this context? Through this lens, we will try to glimpse the complexity of Black migration from within and how institutions like The University of Maryland play a role in the change happening around and within them.

FIGURE 1.2 Excerpts from incubators leader's notes on mapping sessions.

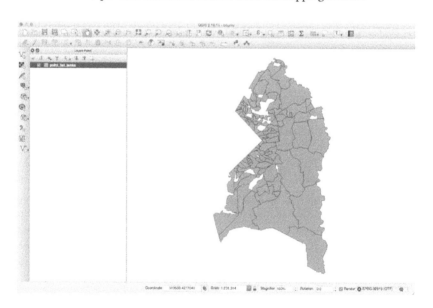

Let's set properties for this layer so that we can see what it can show us.

FIGURE 1.3 A screen capture of a mapping handout for Module 3 of the 2018–2019 Digital Humanities Incubator series.

> In every case, each she/he/they that I describe is, by default, black.
> Refusing to explicitly qualify race in work on black people can be jarring
> because having non-white experiences centered is so rare.
>
> *(Bickerstaff, 2017)*

In other parts of our project, we insisted that our default was Black. But here, we
were bound to prove that the "Black portions" of the archives were valuable and
worthy of digitization. Through our graduate students' work, we had to demonstrate that digitizing these records could yield useful products in the classroom,
furthering university research.

This ultimately was our testbed. The documents, the way the university obtains them, and the mechanisms for acquiring grant funding that often
defaults to digitization as objective served to test our resolve—first to default to
Blackness, however jarring that may be for institutions or funders. And second,
"who we are working for and what we are working towards" (Bickerstaff, 2017).
Documents we digitized went on to find utility by students, instructors and
researchers. For our team, the digitization process gave us a testbed for a praxis
of radical intentionality.

The Intentionally Digital, Intentionally Black *Conference*

The Symposium for Synergies among African American History and Culture and
Digital Humanities was imagined as a conference that would bring together 150
scholars, students, and professionals for a two-day series of workshops, panels, and
presentations. This symposium would "create a national framework for methodological training and a mechanism for generating a national data set" for digital
African American Studies ("Synergies among Digital Humanities and African
American History and Culture: An Integrated Research and Training Model,"
2015, 3). At the time of its writing, the imagined goal was to provide space for
project personnel and university partners to "report on the project methodology and outcomes, demonstrate the tools and methods used, and invite collaboration on ongoing initiatives that develop and initiate a research network for digital
humanities work in African American history and cultural studies." As the time
came to make good on this promise of a symposium, we found once again that the
nature of procuring grant funding at research institutions is often at odds with the
type of radical care and intentionality we aimed to practice. The proposal outlined
a conference that primarily spoke to other institutions. It was designed, by the
grant's original proposal, to raise the university's profile within the digital field; create a methodological canon for Black digital studies; and produce a tangible product for further engagement. In other words, what ultimately was upheld as legible
and important for funders was the ability of research institutions to create space
for intellectual productivity. What we had found in leading and administering
AADHum for three years, however, was a community in search of so much more.

By all accounts the final keystone in AADHum's programming, the conference afforded us one more opportunity to lead with radical Black love, to make choices with care and intentionality, and to strive towards dismantling barriers of access for those who wanted to work within the space of Black and digital studies. This focus reshaped the initial symposium into the development of the *Intentionally Digital, Intentionally Black Conference*—the culmination of AADHum's inaugural years and a loudly declared intervention into the ways of doing digital research and asking humanistic questions. AADHum's four-day conference included a pre-conference workshop day focused on extending the rich work of the DHIs; two days devoted to paper and digital poster sessions showcasing research by members of our growing scholarly community; and, a final day of civic exploration at the Smithsonian National Museum of African American History and Culture (NMAAHC)—known affectionately among Black communities as "The Blacksonian."

As with our other programs, the conference was ultimately about the people, the "collaborative, supportive community of scholars working at the intersection of African American history and culture and the digital humanities" that we had the pleasure of working and building with ("Synergies among Digital Humanities and African American History and Culture: An Integrated Research and Training Model," 2015). As the first Black DH conference of its kind, *Intentionally Digital, Intentionally Black* was also an opportunity to offer a replicable model and establish valuable, thoughtful norms for the field. The themes noted above were reflected through our Statement of Values, choice in facilities, services offered to participants, framework for evaluating paper submissions and panels, and programming decisions.

Early on, we decided that a Statement of Values (see Figure 1.4) could help us set a tone and standard for how we would conduct ourselves as conference planners, how we would protect the most vulnerable members of our community, and how we might guard against the many ways in which institutional policy is often weaponized against Blackness and Black people. We were fortunate to learn from those who have come before us at the Digital Library Federation ("Digital Library Federation (DLF) Code of Conduct," 2017), Geek Feminism Wiki ("Conference Anti-Harassment," 2014), and Humanities Intensive Learning + Teaching Institute ("Statement of Values," 2013), as well as our friend and colleague Dr. Gabrielle Foreman, Ned B. Allen Professor of English and Professor of History and Black American Studies, at the University of Delaware.

Our experiences as scholars of color and as a predominantly female-led staff informed our thinking as much as existing scholarship on the importance of a code of conduct. We have witnessed codes of conduct weaponized against the mere existence of people of color; leveraged to condemn Black intellectual dissent as a threat to white collegiality; and, defanged to privilege civility and "positive" energy of a conference or gathering over the protection of women.

THE AFRICAN AMERICAN HISTORY, CULTURE AND DIGITAL HUMANITIES (AADHUM) INITIATIVE aims to create and hold space for all learners and thinkers exploring the intersections of African American history, culture, and digital humanities. As such, AADHum is dedicated to providing a harassment-free conference experience for everyone regardless of academic status, age, body size, disability, ethnicity, gender, gender identity and expression, origin, physical appearance, sexual orientation, race, or religion. By attending the AADHum conference and any affiliated events, including social gatherings, you signal your commitment to contributing to a safe and inclusive experience for all. We do not tolerate harassment of conference participants in any form.

It is important to understand the range of behaviors that may constitute harassment. Harassment can include, but is not limited to: derogatory verbal comments; sexist, racist, or otherwise discriminatory jokes and language; unwelcome or offensive nonverbal expressions related to physical or cognitive ability, age, appearance, or body size; sexual and/or discriminatory images in public spaces; bullying behavior; deliberate intimidation; stalking; following; harassing photography or recording; questioning someone's right to use the restroom of their choice; sustained disruption of talks or other events; inappropriate physical contact; and unwelcome sexual attention.

This policy is not intended to constrain responsible scholarly or professional discourse and debate. We welcome engagement with difficult topics, practiced with respect and care.

Additionally, AADHum recognizes that codes of conduct such as these often function to accuse Black people–especially Black women–of "threatening" and/or "intimidating" behavior in public spaces. AADHum's effort to value the contributions and participation of all of conference attendees means that the **weaponization of this code to deride, silence, and police Black people will too be considered a violation of this policy.**

Participants asked to stop any harassing behavior are expected to comply immediately. If a participant engages in harassing behavior, the organizers may take any action they deem appropriate. Participants at any conference event, including social events, violating these rules may be sanctioned or expelled from the conference (without refund for conference registration or accompanying events) at the discretion of the

FIGURE 1.4   The Statement of Values that appeared in the AADHum Conference 2018: "Intentionally Black, Intentionally Digital" booklet.

Our AADHum staff frequently traveled to DH workshops, institutes, and trainings within our broader scholarly network. While employed as an instructor for one such workshop, Jessica was harassed several times and targeted for inappropriate comments in public and pedagogical spaces by an older man. Kevin swiftly reported the misconduct, and we learned that our complaints were not the first lodged against this individual. Yet, the workshop administrators made no move to remove or reprimand him, let alone take action to protect Jessica against further harassment. Instead, we were simply reassured that the "code of conduct would be followed" and notified that the annual workshop would next be held at the alleged harasser's home institution. It became clear that the code of conduct would do little to shield Jessica and other attendees from harm; priority was given to the man's comfort, as well as the appearance of collective morale. To redress him—and to affirm Jessica—was to be disruptive to the collective.

We therefore took intentional steps to guard against these all-too-common failings. In the weeks prior to AADHum's conference, it was brought to our attention that a man had been traveling around the world to harass a particular Black scholar for her work on a historical figure. She had documentation from her institution, who recommended that she refrain from attending any more conferences—especially ours, as the man lived in the greater Washington D.C. area. While the recommendation was certainly well-intentioned, it reinforces a frequent refrain: that victims of harassment or abuse are the ones who must sacrifice opportunity in order to provide for their own safety. We quickly began to explore how we could support this scholar, her growth, and her wellbeing. We first offered her an opportunity to share her research virtually, knowing that she might rightfully choose instead to withdraw her presentation altogether. Simultaneously, we began to make plans for her in-person attendance. Kevin immediately informed our Dean's office and requested additional (and unplanned) funds to increase security. Once we confirmed support from the college, we devised a careful plan for how the additional security would be deployed, as we were conscious of what an increased campus police presence would mean for a conference predominantly attended by people of color. Our campus security agreed to remain outdoors and maintain minimal visual presence, while staying actively on-alert for our attendees' needs. Ultimately, our efforts were warranted; the man arrived when the conference began but was met outside by members of our AADHum administrative staff. We immediately alerted campus security and informed the college.

The difference between these two incidents really comes down to care and risk. Radical intentionality is grounded in an ethics of love, and a commitment to assuming the risk for those who deserve to be seen and heard yet are often dismissed or made to carry the burdens of their safety alone. To treat the aggrieved as human is to address issues in ways that declare to them that they are loved, both in private and in public. In both cases, Kevin was there to bear witness to the incidents. In both cases, Kevin's concern rose to a level of action. The difference was in the commitment of the program administrators to providing both structure and support and assuming the risks and full responsibility of protecting the community and its people. What we desired was a transformation in the politics of care.

How to care for the community we were about to call into existence is a question that guided us throughout the conference planning process. Before any participants arrived on campus, we had the opportunity to consider how to solicit participation, make selections, and extend invitations. Our call for participation was purposefully broad, allowing those from various fields to see their work as welcome. Rather than using the term digital humanities, we settled on digital studies. This prompted submissions from sociologists, information studies scholars, journalists and media researchers, and those training in psychology to submit papers, panels, and digital projects. Rather than offer a fully open submission process, we opted for peer review, because we recognize that peer-reviewed conferences are often required for graduate students who wish to pursue internal funding for their attendance. Peer review also allows us to siphon away submissions and studies that treat Black archives or Black people in ways that violated our mission. We asked a cohort of graduate students, faculty, and off-campus researchers to serve on our team for peer review and help us toward foregrounding the work of junior scholars and those who would benefit most from feedback at the conference. These deliberate choices were made with the realities and possibilities of a radically intentional community gathering at the forefront of our minds.

This effort extended to our planning when it came to conference logistics, such as use of on-campus facilities, as well. Cultivating partnerships with the university's Division of Information Technology staff to anticipate basic technical needs helped us to expedite major administrative issues associated with bandwidth distribution and network security. We were also very fortunate to be able to utilize two sites on UMD's campus, both of which allowed us to accommodate participant needs with a quiet room, nursing stations, and all-gender restrooms. The facilities we chose further allowed us to engage in varying types of presentations—some with more traditional furniture arrangement, others set up in a circle to encourage dialogue, and still others prepared as demo sessions to showcase different styles of projects, tools, or skills.

While our memory of that day was a fast, exhausting pace as organizers, we wanted to build a certain slowness into the program. For instance, we scheduled keynote speakers only after breakfast had been offered first, and ensured they could be in conversation with one another and participants after their session. We refrained from overcrowding the program and intentionally organized the schedule to ensure every conference panel would have attendees by utilizing a tiered room capacity system that funneled traffic from well-known panelists to more junior scholars. Several breaks were offered throughout the day, and they always included snacks, coffee, and tea.

In a pre-COVID era, we decided to make livestreaming available for as many presentation sessions as possible through our contacts with the College of Arts and Humanities Classroom Support Team. At the same time, this general commitment to access was navigated with respect for attendees' privacy. Understanding the concerns with intellectual ownership and the terms of service with third-party cloud-based streaming sites such as YouTube, we added an opt-out option on our application form for photography and livestreaming as well. Our team had witnessed a paradigm shift with the use of streaming technology and community building throughout our programming that had led us to believe that cultural norms within the academy around conferencing and streaming were changing in favor of more inclusivity. Most of our participants opted for livestreaming, recognizing the potential to circulate their ideas to a broader audience and reach participants who could not travel to campus for the conference. We were able to host 3,565 views across 12 streams representing the opening plenary, the keynote, and 10 panels over two days.

This conference, like the rest of AADHum programming, was hosted by a team of folks who had attended but never planned an event of this scope before. We made a lot of errors along the way and were grateful to the participants who graciously helped us correct course. The question we encountered most frequently as we departed from AADHum in 2019 was, "will you host another Black DH Conference?" While this team may never do so again together, we hope the radical intentionality that drove each decision behind *Intentionally Digital, Intentionally Black* will inspire other administrators and scholars as the field grows.

FUNDAMENTAL PRINCIPLES OF BLACK DIGITAL HUMANITIES PROGRAMMING

- Black DH must cross the terrain of multiple disciplines while keeping Black folks centered.
- Facilitating conversations in Black DH should create new discussions that we would not see elsewhere.
- Skills instruction in Black DH should be grounded in conversations about Black history, culture, and liberation, prioritizing understandings of technology's impacts on Black life over mastery of tools.
- Support for nascent Black DH projects should make room for experimentation, revision, and playfulness to encourage work that confronts prevailing idioms of racism and racialization, and further extends community to folks whose work would disrupt a tool- or tech-centered approach to DH.
- Digitization efforts for Black DH projects should serve the community of Black scholars and scholarship at institutions receiving funding and the larger Black DH community outside the university or library.
- Black DH gathering places must create opportunities—intellectual, social, and material—for junior scholars that they would not typically find in their disciplinary and institutional homes.

Conclusion

In this chapter, we have outlined AADHum's key programming initiatives. We considered how it is possible to push back (battle) against institutional norms that cause harm to Black students, scholarship, and theory, while simultaneously creating workshops, reading groups, and conferences that re-make Black DH into radically intentional spaces of Black community (build). AADHum was imagined during the Obama administration during a different matrix of possibilities. However, AADHum was implemented during the anxiety of what the 45th president's administration would bring to the work of humanities funding structures and overall consciousness. We battled and built as Jovonne implored because, ultimately, we don't love DH, we love Black folks. AADHum sought to reach out to people and build communities of curiosity, critique, and experimentation with Black people (rather than tools) at the center. This is a radical prospect for a field that too often uses Black history without respect for Black people and culture.

Too often, we find that DH scholarship, books, and conferences are filled with DHers talking to themselves. Long-standing DH centers and scholars exchange resources with one another. However, for those junior scholars looking to establish new ways of approaching digital tools and methods, the entry point is not always clear, and the work is not always welcomed. For senior DH scholars, the language of acquiring funding may be clear, but for newcomers, it is not. For both, we advocate recognition that the language of developing a grant proposal is different than the long and winding path from funding to imagining, building, and sustaining Black DH communities. In the chapters that follow, we chart some of that winding path.

RADICAL REFLECTIONS FOR BUILDING BLACK DH PROGRAMMING

- How can we use Black DH programs to imagine examining the Black experience without making America's racialization project the dominant idiom?
- Have we built in space for conversations and collaborations that exist outside the gaze of whiteness?
- Do your Black BH projects/centers prioritize welcoming people who do not already know how to use and critique tools?
- Does your project/center actively and consistently extend resources to people who have not already had real access to them?
- Does your project/center actively and consistently seek insights and leadership from non-DH folks?
- How does your work protest and resist the language demanded/expected by project funders? How?

Notes

1 Dr. Bickerstaff now serves as a Program Officer for Senior Program Officer for Higher Education Initiatives for The American Council of Learned Societies.
2 If you wish to read Dr. Bickerstaff's essay in full, which was published in early 2017, please see Appendix A. This piece was re-printed with permission from the author and with our thanks and gratitude.
3 Jovonne moderated every event in the AADHum Conversation Series, with the exception of one in which she participated as a panelist. "Black Joy in Arts and Humanities Research" was held in March 2018 at the David C. Driskell Center and moderated instead by Catherine.
4 See Appendix C for the agenda from the first session, which doesn't introduce tools but focuses on artifacts and histories first.

References

African American History, Culture, and Digital Humanities. (2018). *Statement of Values. AADHum Conference 2018: "Intentionally Black, Intentionally Digital" booklet*, College Park, MD.

Bickerstaff, J. (2017, February 18). We who would build: Re-visioning resistance & theorizing beyond the gaze. *African American History, Culture, and Digital Humanities (blog)*. https://web.archive.org/web/20211025065559/https://aadhum.umd.edu/asante/2017/02/centralizing-blackness-digital-work/

Brown, A. M. (2017). *Emergent Strategy : Shaping Change, Changing Worlds*. Chico: AK Press.

Conference Anti-Harassment. (2014, December 29). Geek Feminism Wiki. https://geekfeminism.fandom.com/wiki/Conference_anti-harassment

Digital Library Federation (DLF) Code of Conduct. (2017, October). Digital Library Federation. www.diglib.org/about/code-of-conduct/

Hosbey, J. (2017, February 18). Wake work at the intersection of Black Studies and the Digital Humanities. *African American History, Culture, and Digital Humanities (blog)*. https://web.archive.org/web/20211025065559/https://aadhum.umd.edu/asante/2017/02/centralizing-blackness-digital-work/

Hottle, J. (2013). AFL-CIO President Richard Trumka addresses the history of his organization during the acceptance ceremony on October 1st in front of Hornbake Library. https://history.umd.edu/news/afl-cio-archive-donation-largest-university-maryland-library-history

Maryland Center for Humanities Research (2016). *AADHUM Executive Summary*, Maryland Center for Humanities News. https://arhusynergy.umd.edu/news/aadhum-executive-summary

Statement of Values. (2013). The Humanities Intensive Learning + Teaching (HILT) Institute. http://dhtraining.org/hilt/conferences/values/

Synergies among Digital Humanities and African American History and Culture: An Integrated Research and Training Model. (2015). University of Maryland, College Park, College of Arts and Humanities.

Tompkins, K. W. (2012). *Racial Indigestion*. New York: New York University Press.

2

WHERE ARE ALL THE BLACK SCHOLARS IN BLACK DH?

Creating Space for the Field of Black Digital Studies

Kevin C. Winstead

> Sound is a way to extend the territory you can affect. So people can walk into you way before they can get close to your body. And certainly, the communal singing that people do together is a way of announcing that we're here, that this is real. And so anybody who comes into that space, as long as you're singing, they cannot change the air in that space. The song will maintain the air as your territory.
> —*Bernice Johnson Reagon ("The Songs Are Free: Bernice Johnson Reagon and African-American Music," 1991)*

Sound announces a person's existence before they arrive. For several decades before the field of Black digital studies, there was a community forming—a collective rooted in understanding Black life. Yet, when I entered Black digital studies in 2016, Black Internet Studies (studying Black people being online), Black Data Studies, and Black digital humanities (DH) were distinct disciplinary silos with very little overlap in critical inquiry. As an interdisciplinary scholar whose work spans critical race, social movements, and cultural production, I found the lack of cross-disciplinary engagement antithetical to reading Black life in digital communities and digital tools. Black Studies taught me that investigation into the fullness of Black life is to transgress across disciplinary boundaries in search of the truth. By privileging the subjugated knowledge epistemologies of Black people, we create new pathways for inquiry, rooted in a Black experience, and can critically challenge the digital's lapse into positivistic tendencies to remove one's work from humanity. The community was already building intellectual knowledge. What the African American History, Culture, and Digital Humanities (AADHum) initiative did was leverage access—to the institution's status, financial resources, and social capital—to negotiate multiple domains of

DOI: 10.4324/9781003299134-3

power within the formal knowledge production industry to accelerate the legitimization of Black digital knowledge projects, labor, and scholars.

At the time the first iteration of AADHum disbanded, the field of Black digital studies was listening to that growing sound from various silos and had coalesced multiple disciplines and methodological traditions. This community forged new possibilities under a *Sankofa praxis*, a framework for reaching back to gather the best of Black Studies' intellectual traditions to create new knowledge by reclaiming, reviving, and persevering through the challenges of the modern academy (Alkalimat, 2016). Much like Collins' concept of intellectual activism, a Sankofa praxis resists the privatization and commodification of information and culture and, instead, democratizes intellectual resources—typically gatekept by and within institutions—to support Black people toward developing ideas about how they view themselves and society. This chapter will sketch a timeline of the formation of the intellectual community at the intersections of African American life, culture, and the digital, and explore the lessons AADHum learned in its efforts to support formal recognition of this growing field of inquiry.

Black digital studies is infused by Black scholars with a feminist politics of care to forge new spaces for junior Black scholars to exist. Drawing upon Patricia Hill Collins' matrix of domination and intellectual activism provides a framework for understanding the challenges Black people face when digital studies are institutionalized, as well as their efforts to resist and exist in the face of the privatization of knowledge and the marginalization of Black thought (Collins 2012, 2002). Moya Bailey (2011) also articulates the ways race has informed the creation and recognition of DH fields and the resulting need for corrective measures. Channeling Collins, I recognize how digital studies can exert varying modes of power to shape the social order and how, as a knowledge production enterprise, it reproduces inequality through structural, disciplinary, cultural, and interpersonal domains of power.

I recognize that any story of the intellectual trajectory of Black digital studies is going to be an incomplete one. Regardless of good intentions, any project that tries to trace lineages can intentionally or inadvertently canonize strategic narratives and erase the essential labor of people in the process. Many intellectuals within and outside of the academy have contributed greatly to the field of Black digital studies—including alt-academics, librarians, senior scholars, and graduate students—who have leveraged their time and resources to create space for the community. The field continues to expand its contours at a pace swifter than the speed of publication. Yet, the difficulties of documenting this evolution only further reinforce the significance of doing so. In this chapter, I aim to bear witness to the work of those who have shaped the field and strive to tell the story of how a larger community of intellectuals intentionally created a movement to advance emancipatory knowledge, intellectual validation, and social fellowship.

Black digital studies can be organized from several different perspectives. It is a field that wrestles with the debates it inherited from Africana/African American/

Black Studies and the debates produced by the methodological necessities of doing digital work. Black digital studies encompasses a community of scholars across the disciplinary spectrum. Whether presentist scholars or historians, some study race, racism, and resistance as a mode of inquiry, while others study Blackness both in its mundane and fantastical natures. This community has expanded to include those who pursue Black digital culture studies; Black digital projects, archives, and tools; and university-housed academic centers. Devising an organizing framework that accounts for this diverse range of work and methods is not a clear or simple task. When setting about to organize the activity within this nebulous field, I was first drawn, as a scholar of social movements, to the year 2016.

What's so special about the year 2016? Black scholarship in the U.S. in the mid-2010s was informed by the murder of Trayvon Martin on February 26, 2012, in Sanford, Florida; the rise of the Black Lives Matter movement in Black communities and, much later, mainstream media; and importantly, the end of the Obama administration. In 2016 a shift was signaled in the U.S., both politically and in Black studies scholarship—an intimate connection. I mark this moment as the end of the discourse of American post-raciality and the beginning of an intentional collision between Black Media/Black digital studies and the field of DH. The year also birthed the beginnings of two major events in DH: the Rutgers Digital Blackness conference, which blended Black New Media Studies and Black DH communities; and, the start of AADHum, directed by a scholar who did not emerge from a traditional DH background but, instead, carried forward with her the critical perspectives of a race, communication, and new media scholar.

In the tradition of Black Studies, I read Black digital studies as an intellectual praxis and a social movement grounded in knowledge production. With the year 2016 lingering in my mind, I consider time and change and endeavor to trace the intellectual lineage of Black digital studies, its intervention in the knowledge production of digital studies at large, and the specific practice of legitimization that occurred through the establishment of the nation's first Black digital research center. In doing so, I provide reflections on our existing frameworks for building a critical Black digital community.

KEY QUESTIONS

- How does the history and genealogy of Black digital studies, read alongside and with and the history of community building in Black Studies, inform the future of the field?
- How do institutions serve as boundaries and bridges for scholars in Black DH?
- How can Black digital studies create genuine fellowship for students and faculty at institutions?

The Forefamily

The origin story of Black Studies and social movements teaches us the lesson that the community comes before the field. In order to look toward a future for Black Digital Studies, I begin with a timeline of the formation of the field that points to the importance of community building. Before Black digital studies, there were Black people who expressed identity and found community with each other online through platforms such as USENET, BITNET, and bulletin board platforms (Burkhalter, 1998; McIlwain, 2019). In 1998, Alondra Nelson formed a digital community, Afrofuturism.net, and a mailing list of Black creators, artists, musicians, scholars, and activists. They were focused on crafting a Black fantastic, repurposing Marc Dery's 1993 term "Afrofuturism." On the heels of the rise of Black internet communities came the eBlackStudies initiatives, founded by Abdul Alkalimat, as a call for Black Studies to be responsive to the "virtualization" of the Black experience in the information revolution (2000). The creation of and participation in these and other online communities sparked, for many who would become scholars in the field, the impetus for their studies.

By contrast, other historians, geographers, and statisticians have been using computational tools to analyze Blackness as *a problem* in society for decades. In the early 2000s, emerging scholarship in internet research located race and Blackness as a problem in need of resolution, with a heavy focus on digital divide research. This work focused on racial disparities in African Americans' use of technology. But even as the ideas of the digital divide dominated the field, some Black scholars pushed back by studying ways Black people socially construct *self* and *community* online, creating what André Brock has referred to as *digital Blackness*. The late 1990s and early 2000s saw scholars of popular culture, communication, English, and history pursue research projects on Black cyberculture and race. Academic organizations, such as the Humanities, Arts, Science, and Technology Alliance and Collaboratory (HASTAC), developed in the early half of the 2000s to create space for scholars at the intersection of cultural studies and technology to be in a community with one another.

I identify the first decade of the 21st century as the second wave in the field of Black digital studies, marked by scholarly work that moves away from deficiency models of studying Blackness found in digital divide studies. The second wave of Black digital work, between 2000 and 2010, allowed an interdisciplinary community of scholars to develop graduate research, dissertations, and early scholarship on the study of Blackness/race and cyberculture/digital (Banks, 2003; Barroqueiro, 2003; Becerra, 2010; Brock, 2007; Brockington, 2003; Consilio, 2008; DeWalt, 2010; Funchess, 2008; Lee, 2009; McCormick, 2008; Rice, 2002; Stokes, 2004; Wynn, 2005). The maturation of these scholars formed a new intellectual community in the field of Black digital studies; their efforts carved out the space necessary for future analysis of Black digital cultural production and identity.

The third wave of the scholarship must be contextualized against the backdrop of Web 2.0, online and offline protests, and hashtag social media movements connected to the state-sanctioned murders of Trayvon Martin in 2012, Mike Brown in 2014, Sandra Bland in 2015, and many others. While mainstream media focused heavily, if not exclusively, on images and narrative depictions of Black death and suffering, a younger generation of scholars poured their energy into work centering Black community, joy, creativity, invention, and innovation, and further identified digital spaces as sites of Black life and living. The 2010s welcomed a new group of scholars whose work intentionally infused digital studies with notions of Black feminism and technology (Gray, 2020; Jackson, 2016; Love, 2019; Steele, 2021); Black DH (Bailey, 2011, 2015; Gallon, 2016); Black social media production (Bruns and Burgess, 2011; Clark, 2014; Florini, 2014, 2017); and critical race, data, and technology theory (Benjamin, 2019; McIlwain, 2019; Noble, 2018, 2019). This era in Black digital studies is marked by a definitive reclamation of Black stories as told by Black scholars during the backlash of a failed post-racial narrative in American society. Black digital studies, and Black DH specifically, became projects of recovery. Black digital humanists moved beyond the centralization of tools to name Black DH as a *technology of recovery* where the field makes knowledge more accessible, discoverable, and open for further development and contribution in order "to unmask the racialized systems of power at work in how we understand the digital humanities as a field and utilize its associated techniques" (Gallon, 2016).

As Jessica Marie Johnson (2018a) notes, tracing the formation of Black digital studies acknowledges how Black digital practice reshapes the Black academy. By centering work that did not necessarily come with the validation of the academy, the Black digital studies intellectual community produced new kinds of public scholarship, including the emergence of Black digital syllabi, like the #LemonadeSyllabus (Williams, 2020); community-engaged DH initiatives, such as the Colored Conventions Project (The Colored Conventions Project, 2016); and community-driven data justice projects, such as Documenting the Now (Jules, Summers, and Mitchell, 2018). These projects signal a shift toward digital, crowd-sourced forms of knowledge production and recovery in response to the era of Black Lives Matter; the deadly protests and uprisings in Charleston, Ferguson, and Baltimore; and the Trump presidency.

Yet, in the introduction of *Black Code Studies*, Jessica Marie Johnson and Marc Anthony Neal articulate a frame that pushes beyond the frame of recovery, saying,

> Black Code Studies is queer, femme, fugitive, and radical. As praxis and methodology, it waxes insurgent. It refutes conceptions of the digital that remove black diasporic people from engagement with technology, modernity, or the future. It centers black thought and cultural production across a range of digital platforms, but especially social media, where black freedom struggles intersect with black play and death in polymorphic and polyphonic intimacy.
>
> *(2017, p. 1)*

Johnson and Neal did not seek to create a new field of study; rather, they gave voice to the sounds rumbling in the silos that many interdisciplinary scholars had been privy to for years. Groups such as HASTAC took a deliberate critical race approach in forming identity-focused communities such as #TransformDH in 2011. #TransformDH highlighted the need to analyze both the means of production and the cultural landscape of digital spaces ("About #TransformDH", 2015; Cong-Huyen, 2013). While scholars took an intellectual interest in the role of the digital in Black everyday life, many in the academy had not yet become accommodating to the scholars or the expanding field. Put simply: it was easier to study Black folks as subjects of research than to actually see or embrace them seriously as producers of knowledge.

This is why the work of information studies scholars like Safiya Noble and André Brock are pivotal in establishing the world in which Black digital studies now reside. In 2016, Brock introduced us to Critical Technoculture Discourse Analysis (CTDA), a methodology for studying discourse within digital media spaces that functions independently from algorithmic tools. CTDA argues that, by using a critical cultural theory and analysis of technology's affordances, one can derive a technological artifact's effect on the social. Noble, at the same time, retrains the public's attention on policy, platform, and regulations by bringing the concept of algorithmic bias to the masses. Their work traverses literatures outside of the humanities, reconceptualizing tools for the study of Black culture and supporting greater responsiveness to the impact of technology on the lives and livelihoods of Black folks whom technology touches. When we hosted the 2018 *Intentionally Digital, Intentionally Black* conference, we programmed a keynote conversation between André Brock and Jessica Marie Johnson to force the sounds of that recurring, often-hidden conversation between information studies, humanities, and social sciences into public view.

This work has been intentional, not natural. This long and winding legacy has been continually renewed by scholars who maintain a commitment to centering Black people and Black life in their work and, in doing so, fighting against institutional barriers that persist in marginalizing Black scholars and research. The rise of a potential fourth wave is now being marked by the extension of Black digital research into projects, initiatives, and communities that seek to formally recognize and support a burgeoning canon of scholarship on contemporary Black digital life and culture "in the wake," such as NEH Summer Institutes (Nieves and Gallon); special journal issues (Johnson and Neal); *The Digital Black Atlantic* (Risam and Josephs); research centers (AADHum and DigBlk); and digital archives (DocNow). Demonstrating an increasing institutional commitment to Black DH, the first nationally funded DH cohort was convened by the Mellon CLIR/DLF Postdoctoral Fellowship in Data Curation for African American and African Studies in 2019. I was hired for this role, and the significance of this fellowship—as the hard-earned product of years of intentional community-building and knowledge production—was not lost on me.

This story reminds us that community precedes the field. These scholars, this scholarship, and these sometimes-separate-but-always-interconnected communities provoke a challenge to DH. As Noble (2019) said, "DH work must challenge the impulse in digital humanities that privileges digitality and computerization, along with the related concepts of use, access, and preservation, while often failing to account for more immediate and pressing global concerns" (p. 33). Noble was signaling what we refer to as radical intentionality in building Black DH. Together, we are calling for Black DH—and the centers and initiatives that support them—to generate knowledge about Blackness and about the world using critical Black inquiry, and purposefully aim to change how we participate in and bolster the institutions that reproduce problematic structures of white supremacy.

BLACK DIGITAL STUDIES IN THE U.S.: A TIMELINE

First Wave (< 2000): Community and bulletin board platforms (such as USENET, BITNET, Afrofuturism.net, and eBlackStudies) form and foster Black digital communities

Second Wave (2000~2010): Early dissertations in Black and digital scholarship critique the "digital divide" and spur onward a first generation of scholars engaged in research simultaneously about Blackness, race, and cybercultures

Third Wave (2010~2018): Notions of identity and culture shape Web 2.0, alongside the rise of digital Black activism. Moments of violence and tumult signal the end of American post-raciality narratives and foster increased public visibility of digital Black life that prompt attention to Black DH and emerging centers and initiatives like AADHum

Fourth Wave (2019~present): Black DH attracts institutional investment from grant funders, enabling formally funded community and seeding potential for ongoing intellectual fellowship

---

Institution Building with Radical Intentionality

Collins suggests that the way to empower Black people through the structural domain of power is to transform their institutions. While the scholars doing the community building charted in the preceding section found their scholarship worthy in its own right, institutional validation is an inevitable necessity for enabling a field's growth through graduate education, hiring, retention, and publication. As an interdisciplinary field rather than a discipline, Black digital studies inherits many of the historic, systemic challenges that exist for those who study race and Black culture. There exist tensions, between scholarship and praxis, between varying methodologies, and the structural environments within which Black Studies departments reside. Likewise, we see challenges in equity from funding sources that functionally determine how scholars study Black history and culture (often without Black students and faculty involved).

However, the growing field of Black digital studies as an interdisciplinary community of scholars has a few things working in its favor. As a collection of witnesses in the wake of national discussions of police brutality, Black digital studies follows the tradition of broader Black Studies in maintaining a critical lens on contemporary issues affecting the lives of real people. By centering people over methods, the field is able to transgress disciplinary borders previously maintained between broader digital studies spaces and DH practitioners. Moreover, as a field primarily built by Black scholars, strategic networks of care and sustainability—intentionally formed and navigated in the margins—already exist. As we, therefore, consider the shift from individual, siloed scholars to institutionally funded centers and programs, I am interested in thinking through how we go about transforming institutions for the scholars who need them to do the work of radically intentional Black DH.

I turn our attention first to the *Digital Blackness* Conference at Rutgers University in April of 2016 as a site of institution building. Their Call for Papers reads:

> The 21st century has been marked by the proliferation of access to digital platforms and social media sites that have completely refigured the terms and terrain of racial representation, politics, cultural expression, and scholarly research.
>
> Whether we are speaking of the explosion of web-based series that are distributed through YouTube, the formation of the broad social media community known as Black Twitter, the #BlackLivesMatter movement, or the online Queering Slavery Working Group, profoundly new questions have emerged concerning how the digital has reshaped the meaning, understanding, performance, representation, and reception of Blackness.
>
> What we might call the digital turn also has significant implications for how we study Blackness within and across fields and disciplines. What does Digital Black Studies mean? What are its methodological proclivities and its analytic investments? What are the possibilities of Digital Blackness? What are its limits?
>
> *(Rutgers University, 2015)*

This conference marked the start of a post-2016 era of Black DH that prominently included the voices of those in Black digital media production, as well as scholars in Media and Internet Studies. As an act of institution building, *Digital Blackness* did the critical work of bringing voices from disparate corners of the academy together for conversations about race, Blackness, and digitality. Of the 16 panels, four panels and plenaries were related to race and social media. Four more focused on archiving, preservation, or DH featuring Black archivists and librarians. One such panel, entitled "Digital Black Studies in Practice," featured Neil Fraistat, Bonnie Thornton Dill, Sheri Parks, and Trevor Muñoz—the core architects of what would become AADHum at the University of Maryland.

At the time, I accompanied this group in my capacity as a Graduate Assistant with the University of Maryland Arts and Humanities Center for Synergy and Research. Part of our task was to search for a senior scholar with a traditionally recognizable DH skillset to head this new initiative. Grant-funded centers of this kind typically have senior-level tenured faculty in leadership roles. Yet, the advocacy of senior Black women at the University of Maryland—including Parks, Thornton Dill, and Patricia Hill Collins, none of whom had previous research interests in the digital—inspired the hiring committee to consider a different possibility for this role. Thus, following the *Digital Blackness* conference, Catherine was recruited to direct the first iteration of AADHum in the fall semester of 2016. AADHum would become the first Black DH unit of its kind—not only jointly funded by an external agency and with major institutional support, but also led by a non-DH scholar at its helm. It would further be the first Black DH center to intentionally bring new media studies into the broader DH field. These choices facilitated the first steps down a path toward transforming two institutions: our own university and Black DH more broadly.

The years following the establishment of AADHum brought even more institutionalization of Black digital studies and Black DH, as we pursued efforts to build relationships with other Black scholarly and intellectual communities. Among them was Data for Black Lives (D4BL), a collection of scholars, activists, mathematicians, and organizers that came together in 2017 with the mission to use data science to create change in the lives of Black people. AADHum sent me to their conference in January 2019 to make on-ground connections, and D4BL has since hosted multiple conferences and brought folks together to create white papers and circulate curricula and other resources to push for change at the policy and institutional levels. Humanities Intensive Learning and Teaching (HILT) Institute has thrived since 2013 as a week-long training institute that includes skills-ground workshops and keynote talks for researchers, students, early career scholars, and cultural heritage professionals who seek to learn more about DH theory, practice, and culture. Beginning in 2016, sessions with a focus on Black life and culture have included: "Introduction to the Text Encoding Initiative (TEI) for Black Digital Humanities" with Jessica Lu and Caitlin Pollock; "Black Spatial Humanities" with Kim Gallon; "Black Publics in the Humanities: Critical and Collaborative DH Projects, Spaces and Stories in the Black Public Humanities" with Jim Casey and Sarah Patterson of the Colored Conventions project; and "Developing Black Digital Humanities Initiatives" with Trevor Muñoz and Catherine Knight Steele. Each of these sessions weaves together traditional training with institutional development practices that attendees can bring back to their home institutions.

AADHum had, at its core, an institutional directive to

> bring together work and research in African American and digital human-
> ities in order to expand upon both fields, making the digital humanities
> more inclusive of African American history and culture and enriching
> African American studies research with new methods, archives, and tools.
> *("Synergies among Digital Humanities and African American History and*
> *Culture: An Integrated Research and Training Model," 2015)*

This charge was a direct response to the growing intellectual community I have
already described above. But, in assuming leadership of AADHum in practice,
we interpreted this directive as both an effort and opportunity to see and recognize the kind of scholars and scholarship emerging in a post-Travon, post-
Ferguson, post-Obama era that were modeling and demanding intentionality
within Black DH projects.

In our view, the birth of AADHum was in and of itself a radically intentional
declaration: it is not enough to study Black history or cultural artifacts with
digital tools. Students and scholars were calling upon this burgeoning field to
consider how its resources, tools, and scholarship could hold power to account.
By building on the legacy of Black Studies, we might radically transform our
institutions through our scholarship. I propose that there is a throughline from
the political landscape of this time to the transformation of Black DH. The
acceptance of social media analysis and media studies into the field signaled a
necessary shift, from the margins to the center, of Black DH within DH writ
large. Black DH has consistently and loudly given voice to scholarship that challenges and transforms the discipline.

Such transformations have been fueled by emerging and junior scholars. As
we began the work at AADHum through programming like Reading Groups,
Conversation Series, and Digital Humanities Incubators, we saw a demand from
graduate students who wanted to be trained in methods, exposed to cross-disciplinary scholarship, and given legitimacy and latitude to develop digital-focused
dissertation projects. Our students, both within our community and across the
nation, were often entering their work in closer alignment with the positionality
of the *Digital Blackness* conference than traditional DH scholarship—meaning
their sites of inquiry often prioritized digital platforms and digital representation.
Many of these students had not previously considered how digital humanists'
methods could enhance inquiry into studies of race and identity. This distinction
put our given mission at odds with our lived experience.

We found ourselves in a moment where we needed to resist the institutional
forces at play. On the one hand, we had to recognize and respect that our community had long been disciplined by the cultural and methodological distinctions
that mark requirements of advancement in their home fields; on the other hand,
we sought to play and experiment across disciplinary boundaries in ways that

helped students and scholars point to AADHum and Black DH as a *real*, legitimate, institutionally legible thing. I draw your attention to a student on our campus who worked and learned alongside us for years. Her work would now very clearly be described and recognized as fitting in the framework of Black digital studies. However, because her disciplinary home had not previously seen or treated digital scholarship as valid, she struggled to find community and support for the work she did. She needed the institution first to validate her work, so that she could work towards transforming the institution through her scholarship. (It's important to note that this was not just an intellectual imperative; it was a material one. Without the validation of her home department, she could not move forward as a graduate student; her funding and institutional affiliation was always on the line.) In AADHum, she found resources and opportunities that helped her make a case for her work for those who were stubbornly still unconvinced. She attended and later, led workshops for AADHum and invited her department to co-sponsor events. By the end of her time at the University of Maryland, her department recognized her Black DH scholarship as groundbreaking in the field. She wrote critical work about violence against Black women and, through her dissertation, rewrote histories of Black feminist thought by using digital tools and studying social media.

Turning our attention to this example also reminds us that the status quo of rewarding and privileging the tenure-track and already-tenured community above all others is in conflict with our assessment of how to build this space. Building a faculty who are attentive to and care about Black DH is imperative in institution building. We advocate strongly for tenure lines and promotion guidelines that account for the differentiated kind of scholarship (databases, maps, tools) that may be produced within the realm of digital inquiry. These faculty can and do produce research and lead teaching efforts that enliven a new generation of scholars and scholarship. Yet, too often, an over-focus on faculty research and hiring can distract us from the truth of how institutions can best serve Black DH. In the history I detailed above, most of the scholars whose work built the foundations of Black DH did so in defiance of their disciplinary homes. In many cases, they produced work that prompted skepticism from their committees, advisers, and peers; they had to convince them that their work was viable and valuable within the confines of their disciplines, and, most often, they undertook this burden as graduate students.

My own position as a graduate student while working for AADHum—hired even before the director was recruited and brought onto the grant—provided unique insight into the institution's perspective during the formation of the initiative and throughout its public programming. I never felt bound to my institution, but I did understand that my own success—and that of the AADHum—relied on my ability to navigate the constraints and expectations of the institution and to create institutional buy-in for my work. For any student interested in navigating a similar path, I encourage an honest assessment of where the boundaries exist in your own institution, where you can challenge those boundaries, and where you might find allies and advocates willing to help chart the course of radical transformation from within.

But also, for those of us who make it to the other side, we must ask: once the work of Black DH becomes a part of the institution, once individuals have broken free from their silos, how does the sound change? How do we create new pathways for students so they can imagine, build, and write without having to convince anyone of the viability of their work? How can Black DH centers and initiatives prompt the institution to serve this population by legitimizing, validating, and supporting their efforts? How can students and early career scholars continue to merge the traditions of DH and digital studies—with Black Studies ever-present at the core—in ways that allow them to pursue scholarship that has positive material consequences for Black lives *and* their own intellectual and professional pursuits? Through our work with AADHum, I propose an answer: with radical intentionality in remembering, extending, and paying tribute to the caregiving labor of the forefamily, we can leverage the institution as a bridge toward real fellowship, rather than a boundary against and between the advancement of students and scholars.

Actualizing the Intellectual Fellowship

Through our discussion of AADHum's programming in the preceding chapter and the radical attention toward care and teaching that Catherine and Jessica outline in the two that follow, we can see how separate individuals can become a community of scholars. However, as we considered our charge at AADHum—doubly bound to the institution and the ever-growing radical community of Black Studies and Black DH thinkers—we recognized that fellowship doesn't *just happen*. There are ethical practices, specifically regarding resource allocation, that helps sustain the community through intentionally designed intellectual fellowship. Engaging in radically intentional intellectual activism calls upon scholars and public intellectuals to assess the meaning of their work. For grants, initiatives, and centers, that requires us to think through the significance of the spaces we create and the role we play in redirecting funds for community building and intellectual projects. That reflection can happen in the proposal phase where we are required to detail how we will use grant funds to perform operations. But, more often, it happens as we adjust and make changes to our plans to fit the needs of the community in real-time, as the collective forms, develops, and grows. For AADHum, we considered how our stewardship of institutional funding could impact scholars, community, and other entities beyond our campus and outside of academia—those who otherwise do not receive recognition, legitimacy, or financing for their work.

Indeed, a very real part of the work of the humanities is to put financial resources in the hands of people doing the good work. Beyond wielding the capacity to call community into existence, formally established centers are also capable of shaping the environment in such a way that creates truly a safe intellectual space for scholarly exchange. For example, AADHum co-sponsored a one-day symposium at UMD, "Space, Race, Place, and Digital Mapping," which introduced participants to various DH methods and resources on our campus, including the Michelle Smith Collaboratory for Visual Culture. Participants also engaged in a series of dialogues on digital mapping to learn how DH shed light on pervasive facets of systemic inequality in America. As part of that symposium, we partnered with the department of Sociology to host policy analyst and justice activist Samuel Siyangwe from the *Mapping Police Violence* project. Siyangwe's presentation revolved around how data visualization is useful in creating policy narratives for change. He discussed the continued need for resources to help activists and analysts, who often donate their time and labor. Providing space for this dialogue within the context of our newly formed AADHum initiative provided three distinct opportunities for fellowship. First, it allowed us to name Samuel and the work he did within the tradition of Critical Race and DH, opening possibilities for others on campus interested in this work to see AADHum as a potential home for connection and support. This event also provided an example of the utility of the humanities in both policy and social science work, further demonstrating the promising elasticity of the field. Black digital studies had not only grown but had shifted in focus for a new generation of scholars anxious to use DH tools for justice. And, finally, it reminded us that when we have the means, we can purposefully and intentionally choose to put those financial resources in the hands of a justice activist. We often think of an "intellectual community" as a group of like-minded researchers with similar interests and methods. However, for us, a radically intentional intellectual fellowship involves more than our scholarly projects. It is about the quality of fellowship, sociality, and human condition of the scholars themselves.

Perhaps our greatest example of active attention towards fellowship comes from our *Intentionally Digital, Intentionally Black* conference. We used the conference name as the first signal to participants that Black digital studies, as a field and intellectual fellowship, would be prioritized by this institution and in this space. The title reflects an invitation to the various disciplinary backgrounds in this growing field—including Sociology, Information Studies, New Media, Kinesiology, and Popular Culture—to connect meaningfully with traditional DH spaces in history, English, and Archival Studies. This moment marks a rapid recognition of Black DH as a field that both engages with and moves independently from broader DH history, theory, and practice.

In "All of the Digital humanists are White, All the Nerds Are Men, but Some of Us Are Brave," Moya Bailey (2011) reminds us that being Black, or doing work that engages Black culture, at digital studies conferences can often feel alienating. While many of the most prominent conference spaces have acknowledged the lack of diverse voices, it is difficult to break away from dynamics that cause hypersegregation, which is often replicated and reinforced through institutional routines and "best practices." Even as event organizers seek ways to diversify those spaces, interactions at the micro- and interpersonal levels remain hostile, harmful, and alienating. Radical intentionality means making conscious decisions to change those everyday interpersonal interactions by thinking both about the factors that enable them and those that would instead foster intellectual fellowship.

As Jessica Marie Johnson noted during her keynote address at the *Intentionally Digital, Intentionally Black* conference,

> we don't have a space for those who are doing Black and digital things to come together and … it's phenomenal because this conference has been done in a way that has been not just intentionally black and digital, but also intentional in care and spaces for quiet breaks and really good food—which is rare in academic space and something I normally see in organizer type spaces.
>
> (Johnson, 2018b)

Johnson's words allow us to reflect on the business of conferencing as a praxis of care. Indeed, what we aimed to do was revive and build upon the spirit of Black communal gatherings—both within and beyond the academy—that preceded us, while also intentionally deconstructing the disciplinary divides that Black Studies transgresses.

According to the official grant proposal documents, our charge was to host a two-day national symposium for a projected 150 attendees during the final quarter of 2018, to allow project and institutional partners "to report on the project methodology and outcomes, demonstrate the tools and methods used, and invite collaboration on ongoing initiatives that develop and initiate a research network for digital humanities work in African American history and cultural studies" ("Synergies among Digital Humanities and African American History and Culture: An Integrated Research and Training Model," 2015). This was a lofty ask for a staff that had no experience whatsoever in conference planning. The demands were made even more difficult by the stated budget, which did not exceed $20,000 and was meant to cover all costs, including those related to honoraria, travel, and accommodations for two keynote speakers; morning and afternoon coffee breaks each day; a closing reception; and rentals for spaces, furniture, and technical equipment and support. Anyone with experience in conference planning should plainly see that these plans did not respect the materials or labor necessary to facilitate and support true, substantive fellowship; instead, it assumed that merely putting people in a room was enough. And perhaps it would have been if our aim was simply to trade ideas about tools, engage in self-promotion, or facilitate the exchange of business cards with impressive institutional affiliations imprinted on them. For that, we could have easily outsourced the work of conference planning to our university's existing conference planners.

Instead, we had to tap into an unanticipated resource—our own commitment to radical intentionality in centering the people—to allocate limited resources in ways that would transform the institutional practices of conferencing into a mechanism for productive and nourishing fellowship. As a project manager, I took one look at the budget and knew that administering a culturally appropriate conference—one that was enriching, affirming, joyful, and sociable—would require us to leverage our institution and community networks; apply culturally specific tactics of making a dollar out of 15 cents; and being creative about reimagining the resources around us. Sometimes, that means channeling a survivor's epistemology. Every time I knocked on the door of a colleague, traded a favor for necessary supplies, or reconnected with an acquaintance who knew somebody who knew somebody, I drew on the spirit of a Black feminist refugee epistemology, which asserts that institutional disciplinary power is about disruption and displacement, but also replication. Through our critique, creativity, and ability to forge anew what was once old, we can create new ways of being (Davis, 1998; Espiritu and Duong, 2018; Speight Vaughn, 2020; Woods, 2009). Our role as agents of care was to stand in between what is and what is possible.

We do not mean to suggest that the limitations of the grant proposal were nefarious or intentionally short-sighted. At the start of the project, I do not believe the grant's principal investigators could imagine the importance that a space like this could hold, even just three years later. The rapid development of the field, the creation of a local community of Black DH scholars, and the network that had emerged surprised us, as well. If anything, the budgetary constraints embedded in the initial proposal bring into sharp relief the ways in which funders rely upon the resources of already-established institutions to subsidize the costs of grant work. The real conference budget required to meet the needs of our growing AADHum community could have easily exceeded $30,000; yet, the costs would have been even higher for a smaller and less funded institution. We were fortunate as a research-one flagship university; our institution wielded power over spaces that could be used to accommodate our conference needs and was additionally connected with sponsors with much stronger influence than we possessed. Our proximity to Washington D.C. and Baltimore also meant that we could point participants to multiple travel options into the city and several lodging options beyond our official offerings. Our university also owns and operates an alumni center readily equipped for conference needs; a theater and performance facility; a new building designed to support classroom innovation and pedagogical technologies; and conference hotels located on and adjacent to campus. It is impossible to separate AADHum from the institution that houses it; such may be the case for the centers and initiatives that follow in its footsteps. A radically intentional approach continually asks: even, and especially when we don't have all that we need, how can we strategically channel and (re)direct the varied resources at our disposal toward supporting good work and the people who pursue it?

By intentionally seeking and acquiring additional support at the college level, co-sponsorship funds, and a tier-based registration fee, we were able to not only cover the cost for all 250 registrants but also provide need-based travel awards for students. With an overwhelming majority of the remaining funds dedicated to food alone, it is clear how our staff interpreted the grant proposal's original charge. For us, the conference was more than just an opportunity to trumpet the institutional successes of the initiative; it was a chance for our people to gather, to join in raising their voices loudly as a collective, and to elevate the sonic pleasure of an ever-growing Black DH community above the din of disciplinary constraints and rhythms. We aimed to make the conference *feel* right for the intellectual fellowship we so earnestly hoped to serve by recognizing and providing for attendees' physical and material needs.

Beyond demanding a reorientation to how we approach funding with radical intentionality, the notions of fellowship I center here prompt attention to Black faith traditions. Fellowship in the Black faith tradition offers spiritual comfort, a sense of community, and moral guidance. While working for AADHum, I saw the potential in initiatives, grants, and centers to offer a sense of like-minded community, belonging, and a place to openly and honestly discuss the realities of existing in traditionally white spaces. Prioritizing fellowship, and marking it as a critical next step in building toward a field of Black digital studies, impacted our thinking on issues of openness and access.

We worked to make our programming and conference available to publics who are not usually unable to attend campus physically, not only due to geography but also due to historic barriers that prohibit Black and brown people from moving freely throughout the world. Though we were situated at a land-grant public institution, we all know that universities, labeled "free" and "open to the public," are hardly universally accessible. Even those who traverse paths nearby our campus might still meet roadblocks—physical and otherwise—based on a variety of factors, including: access to reliable public transportation, scheduling of events during traditional business hours, mobility concerns and hindrances, cost of travel and parking, and the ugly legacies of our institution (and many others) as unwelcoming to the same communities that surround and support them. Years before the first whispers of COVID-19 reached us and a global pandemic prompted an academy-wide effort to make virtual learning and engagement more manageable, we sought to lower barriers to access by recording presentations, talks, and events whenever it did not jeopardize the intellectual or physical safety of our participants. We pushed for an online experience that would make fellowship possible for those unable to attend in person.

It was a community-focused effort, through and through; I cultivated relationships with our college's Academic Technology and Administrative Operations team (Kathleen Cavanaugh, Nathaniel Kuhn, Monica Milstead), who aided us in developing our livestream technology to make scholarship and engagement a much more inclusive process. Livestreaming afforded us a public video archive for our events and the *Intentionally Digital, Intentionally Black* conference. Not only did this increase the exposure for our participant scholars and practitioners who were accomplishing groundbreaking work in the field, but it also contributed to our loud declarations: that we, as a scholarly community, exist and there is value in bringing us together to share ideas.

In one respect, what we were called to do with AADHum is nothing new for Black communities within the academy. We can look to the histories of the Association for the Study of African American Life and History (ASLAH), the Association of Black Sociologists, and so many other Black scholarly associations, and see that Black intellectual communities have always been charged—whether explicitly or not—with changing the conversation about race and Black life. Much like the organizations that preceded us, we took up the mantle to provide space for the exchange of ideas—speaking truth to people, and to power. With radical intentionality, we leveraged the resources of our institutions to see, affirm, and reach out to Black communities who remain committed to Black life and culture.

KEY LESSONS: CENTERS, INSTITUTIONS, AND INTELLECTUAL ACTIVISM

Intellectual activism is "the myriad ways that people place the power of their ideas in service to social justice" (Collins, 2012, ix). It includes speaking truth to power and speaking truth to the people. **Speaking truth to power** includes pushing back against the status quo in academia, while **speaking truth to people** means making one's academic knowledge and methods available beyond the institutional barriers including gatekeeping, paywalls, and academic journals.

Intellectual activism and centers provide unique infrastructure for resisting local, institutional pressure towards insular silos. Centers can provide unique opportunity for multiple modes of community, by providing access, recognition, and legitimacy for minority scholars; creating opportunity for civic communities to be included and engaged in research ideation, design, and process; enabling access products of scholarly work through public humanities engagement; and, sharing financial resources to community-led projects through seed funding, honorariums, and awards. Centers must approach their budgets as opportunities to (re) allocate resources to community stewards, activists, and organizations.

Radical Reflections for Field- and Fellowship-Building

Black Digital Studies is a multidisciplinary field that is built in the image of Black life. Reading the field as a movement, its genesis can be found in Black people building sites of community online and in everyday life, where a first-generation of Black digital scholars participated and simultaneously sounded the alarm that these communities were worth studying. As intellectual interests in Black digital life and culture grew, and emerging technologies facilitated new modes of inquiry, the scholarly community expanded its intellectual side projects into full-blown dissertations and full-length manuscripts. AADHum, like other emerging centers and initiatives, has aided in the institutionalization of digital studies research, charged with cultivating scholarly interest and community focused on Black digital inquiry.

Reflecting on AADHum's work, we realize that the critical mass of energy for Black Digital studies resides within graduate students and people whose research agendas are more flexible and open to adaptation, playfulness, and risk-taking than the traditional tenure track permits. We aimed to leverage our position within the academic landscape to build an institution that honored and paid tribute to the communities that preceded it and made it possible— that made interventions in the broader field of DH that our Black forefamilies could be proud of. With radical intentionality, we aimed to speak truth to power and to speak truth to people; first, by course-correcting our focus on community to include public intellectuals, community organizations, and an international community of graduate students; and second, by thinking through what it meant to legitimize a field by acknowledging Black scholars and their work, providing financial and intellectual networks, and rethinking how we increase access, documentation, and circulation of scholarship for multiple publics. By centering Black life, we can make digital inquiry, tools, and methods more available to new voices. We create more space for the sounds of Black people and Black culture to echo throughout and beyond the academy.

Creating this space means doing the work of legitimizing marginalized voices but also providing opportunities for that community to be in dialogue with each other on how to navigate the world. It's like the song "Wade in the Water." Bernice Johnson Reagon tells us that every song has multiple meanings depending on the singer's intentions. For some listeners, wading in the water can be heard as a song of jubilee, a performance of joy and affirmation. For some, wading in the water can be the song of fellowship or how to pass along the strategies and tactics for survival. It can also mean how to move from one place to another, where fulfillment and hope are realized. AADHum provided us the opportunity to sit with these purposes simultaneously. We believe centers, initiatives, and grant-funded projects enjoy a unique opportunity within the academy to find ways for multiple needs and desires to collide with and confirm one another—to create a seemingly impossible harmony and issue, once more, a refrain that trumpets love, life, and care for Black people.

RADICAL REFLECTIONS FOR FIELD- AND FELLOWSHIP-BUILDING

- How can I leverage the resources—including social capital and reputation—and of my institution to create, support, and/or legitimize community?
- How do we use our situated privileged to position ourselves as advocates for our imagined communities?
- How do you stand between what is *and* what is possible?
- How do you build within institutions while honoring culture?
- How am I pushing against institutional norms to make space for people?
- How can I reframe public engagement as essential to intellectual fellowship?

References

About #TransformDH. (2015, July 6). TransformDH. https://transformdh.org/about-transformdh/

Alkalimat, A. (2000). eBlack studies: A twenty-first-century challenge. *Souls*, 2(3), 69–76.

Alkalimat, A. (2016, December 1). The Sankofa principle: From the drum to the digital. *30th Symposium on African American Culture and Philosophy*, Purdue University African American Studies and Research Center.

Bailey, M. (2011). All the digital humanists are white, all the nerds are men, but some of us are brave. *Journal of Digital Humanities*, 9(2). http://journalofdigitalhumanities.org/1-1/all-the-digital-humanists-are-white-all-the-nerds-are-men-but-some-of-us-are-brave-by-moya-z-bailey/

Bailey, M. (2015). #transform(ing) DH writing and research: An autoethnography of digital humanities and feminist ethics. *DHQ: Digital Humanities Quarterly*. www.digitalhumanities.org/dhq/vol/9/2/000209/000209.html

Banks, A. J. (2003). Transformative access: An African American rhetoric of technology (Doctoral dissertation, The Pennsylvania State University)

Barroqueiro, T. (2003). Spirit of the digital age: The synergy of cyberculture and hip-hop (Doctoral dissertation, Fordham University). https://research.library.fordham.edu/dissertations/AAI13851636

Becerra, M. D. (2010). Relationships of masculinity and ethnicity as at-risk markers for online sexual addiction in men (Doctoral dissertation, Texas A&M University-Commerce).

Benjamin, R. (2019). *Race after technology: Abolitionist tools for the New Jim Code*. John Wiley & Sons.

Brock, A. (2007). Race, the Internet, and the hurricane: A critical discourse analysis of Black identity online during the aftermath of Hurricane Katrina (Doctoral dissertation, University of Illinois at Urbana-Champaign).

Brockington, W. G. (2003). African-American college students and internet use: A study of uses and gratifications (Doctoral dissertation, Howard University).

Bruns, A., & Burgess, J. E. (2011, August 27). The use of Twitter hashtags in the formation of ad hoc publics. *Proceedings of the 6th European Consortium for Political Research (ECPR) General Conference 2011*. University of Iceland, Reykjavik. https://eprints.qut.edu.au/46515/

Burkhalter, B. (1998). Reading race online. In Peter Kollock and Marc Smith (Eds.), *Communities in cyberspace* (pp. 60–75). Psychology Press.

Clark, M. D. (2014). To tweet our own cause: A mixed-methods study of the online phenomenon. Black Twitter (Doctoral dissertation, The University of North Carolina at Chapel Hill).

Collins, P. H. (2002). *Black feminist thought: Knowledge, consciousness, and the politics of empowerment* (10th ed.). Routledge.

Collins, P. H. (2012). *On intellectual activism*. Temple University Press.

Cong-Huyen, A. (2013, January). #mla13 thinking through race. *Modern Language Association Convention 2013*, Boston, MA. https://anitaconchita.wordpress.com/2013/01/07/mla13-presentation/

Consilio, J. (2008). Attitudes of African American vernacular speakers towards technology (Doctoral dissertation, Purdue University).

Davis, A. Y. (1998). *Blues legacies and Black feminism: Gertrude Ma Rainey, Bessie Smith, and Billie Holiday*. Pantheon Books.

DeWalt, M. R. (2010). Reinventing black: Digital media as a catalyst for changes in identity and social race perceptions of African Americans (Doctoral dissertation, Prescott College).

Espiritu, Y. L., & Duong, L. (2018). Feminist refugee epistemology: Reading displacement in Vietnamese and Syrian refugee art. *Signs: Journal of Women in Culture and Society*, *43*(3), 587–615.

Florini, S. (2014). Recontextualizing the racial present: Intertextuality and the politics of online remembering. *Critical Studies in Media Communication*, *31*(4), 314–326.

Florini, S. (2017, October 10). *Oscillating networked publics: Contingent uses of Black digital networks*. Digital Dialogue, Maryland Institute for Technology in the Humanities. http://mith.umd.edu/dialogues/dd-fall-2017-sarah-florini/

Funchess, J. M. (2008). African Americans in the information age: Challenges and social adaptations (Doctoral dissertation, Wayne State University).

Gallon, K. (2016). Making a case for the Black digital humanities. *Debates in the Digital Humanities*, 42–49. https://dhdebates.gc.cuny.edu/read/untitled/section/fa10e2e1-0c3d-4519-a958-d823aac989eb

Gray, K. L. (2020). *Intersectional tech: Black users in digital gaming*. LSU Press.

Jackson, S. J. (2016). (Re)Imagining intersectional democracy from Black feminism to hashtag activism. *Women's Studies in Communication*, *39*(4), 375–379.

Johnson, J. M. (2018a). Markup bodies: Black [life] studies and slavery [death] studies at the digital crossroads. *Social Text*, *36*(4), 57–79.

Johnson, J. M. (2018b, October). AADHum conference keynote presentation. *"Intentionally Digital, Intentionally Black" AADHum Conference 2018*, University of Maryland.

Johnson, J. M., & Neal, M. A. (2017). Introduction: Wild seed in the machine. *The Black Scholar 47*(3), 1–2.

Jules, B., Summers, E., & Mitchell, V. (2018). Documenting the Now white paper: Ethical considerations for archiving social media content generated by contemporary social movements. Documenting the Now. www.docnow.io/docs/docnow-whitepaper-2018.pdf

Lee, J. E. R. (2009). "A threat on the Net": Stereotype threat in avatar-represented online groups (Doctoral dissertation, Stanford University). www.learntechlib.org/p/122461/

Love, A. (2019). Digital Black feminism. In D. C. Parry, C. W. Johnson, & S. Fullagar (Eds.), *Digital dilemmas: Transforming gender identities and power relations in everyday life* (pp. 53–71). Springer International Publishing.

McCormick, M. (2008). African American girls on MySpace: Artistic expression, viral marketing and corporate presence (Doctoral dissertation, Arizona State University).

McIlwain, C. D. (2019). *Black software: The internet and racial justice, from the AfroNet to Black Lives Matter.* Oxford University Press.

Noble, S. U. (2018). *Algorithms of oppression: How search engines reinforce racism.* NYU Press.

Noble, S. U. (2019). Towards a critical black digital humanities. In *Debates in the digital humanities.* https://dhdebates.gc.cuny.edu/read/untitled-f2acf72c-a469-49d8-be35-67f9ac1e3a60/section/5aafe7fe-db7e-4ec1-935f-09d8028a2687

Reagon, B. J. (1991). *The songs are free: Bernice Johnson Reagon and African-American Music.* Films Media Group. https://fod.infobase.com/PortalPlaylists.aspx?wID=107812&xtid=6774

Rice, J. R. (2002). The rhetoric of cool: Computers, cultural studies, and composition (Doctoral dissertation, The University of Florida).

Rutgers University. (2015). *CFP: Digital Blackness Conference.* New Brunswick, NJ. https://networks.h-net.org/node/5293/discussions/74691/cfp-digital-blackness-conference-april-22-3-2016-new-brunswick.

Speight, M. V. (2020). Black epistemologies and blues methodology: Engaging liminal ontological space in qualitative research. *Qualitative Inquiry: QI, 26*(8–9), 1090–1101.

Steele, C. K. (2021). *Digital Black feminism.* New York University Press.

Stokes, C. E. (2004). Representin' in cyberspace: Sexuality, hip hop, and self-definition in home pages constructed by Black adolescent girls in the HIV/AIDS era (Doctoral dissertation, University of Michigan).

The Colored Conventions Project. (2016). The Colored Conventions Project. http://coloredconventions.org/

University of Maryland, College of Arts and Humanities. (2015). *Synergies among digital humanities and African American History and culture: An integrated research and training model.* Andrew W. Mellon Foundation.

Williams, S. (2020). The Black digital syllabus movement: The fusion of academia, activism and arts. *Howard Journal of Communications, 31*(5), 493–508.

Woods, C. (2009). Katrina's world: Blues, bourbon, and the return to the source. *American Quarterly, 61*(3), 427–453.

Wynn, A. (2005). Control, alt, delete: African Americans escaping the digital divide (Doctoral dissertation, American University).

3

WHAT ARE WE GOING TO EAT?

Care and Feeding as Radical Method and Praxis

Catherine Knight Steele

Our last African American History, Culture, and Digital Humanities Initiative (AADHum) team meeting was a brunch at Miss Shirley's Restaurant in Baltimore. I marveled at my good fortune to work with this group over the previous three years. We reflected on our work as we laughed over crab cakes and cheese grits. But more importantly, we reflected on the space we created to sustain ourselves and the folks whose work we were so fortunate to touch over the past three years.

Our team was comprised of scholars who approached DH from very different perspectives. For example, some considered hashtags as mechanisms to trace online activism, while others wrote about security and privacy issues online. In contrast, others drew upon digitized records from the 19th century to consider the ideological work of building arguments around freedom for the newly emancipated. Within this group, trained in different methods, we developed a synergy, not simply around how we would provide activities for our community of scholars but also how we would choose to engage in a radically intentional praxis of care—both with each other and with our research. I cannot help but think that, in part, some of this deep commitment to care in our stewardship of AADHum was forged by the way we cared for one another through food.

I remember early on in our team's experience as a unit how frequently my colleagues would remind me and each other to stop, slow down, and eat. It was more than a reflection of my medical need to maintain my blood sugar levels; it established a norm of inviting one another to situate our own needs as critical to the success of the grant. Our team's foodways quickly expanded beyond the snacks in our desk drawers and work bags to intentional time at our weekly meeting devoted to lunch and community. We always began our weekly team meetings with a question: "what are we going to eat?" From there, someone

DOI: 10.4324/9781003299134-4

was usually tasked with ordering for the group—soul food, Thai, Jamaican? The cuisine changed weekly. However, the commitment to making sure we were all fed did not. Psyche Williams-Forson (2021) explains, "Food is a demarcation of group identity, so what is consumed and the choices made surrounding that consumption speak volumes about individuals and community identity" (p. 89).

When we first began our weekly meeting in our new office, one team member, Jessica, brought her lunch. Before we developed an intimacy as a group, we individually speculated as to why she did not often order food with us. Did she not like take-out? Did she prefer healthier options? Did she follow a strict budget? But as trust built among our group over our long lunches, we found out Jessica brings her lunch because the food she makes at home is far better than anything we could order. So, it was not long before Jessica welcomed us to her home to experience her homemade phở or brought in mango pie to share at the end of a long day. Williams-Forson (2021), citing Claude Grignon, explains that consumption of food and drinks "activates and tightens internal solidarity, but it happens because commensality first allows the limits of the group to be redrawn, its internal hierarchies to be restored, and is necessary to be redefined" (p. 89). Indeed, as we ate and communed with one another, we redrew our lines of formality and hierarchy—all hungry, all fed, all contributing to the care and feeding of one another.

Therefore, it was no surprise that when it came time to plan *Intentionally Digital, Intentionally Black*, the first international Black digital humanities (DH) conference, our team had one primary requirement: to feed the people who came to share their work with us. We would feed them breakfast and lunch, and we would arrange snacks in between sessions. We would consider their dietary needs. We would provide the time and the physical space for folks to sit and eat without being rushed to move between sessions. We would open rooms for folks to decompress alone, even as we ensured that meals provided time to be in community with one another. We also forged relationships with staff on campus who, because of their own cultural understanding of feeding and care, ensured that the food we provided would feel less like standard conference fare and more like home. We forcefully advocated for feeding our guests, sometimes finding ourselves in conflict with other administrators who believed too much time or energy was going into those parts of the conference planning. However, what we knew—not intuitively, but because of our commitment to prioritize care—was that none of the good work of Black DH would be possible or meaningful if it was not intentionally enabled by care and feeding for all.

Ethics of care first emerged in feminist scholarship in the 1980s when Carol Gilligan (1977) forcefully pushed back against the public sphere, universal moralism, and justice-oriented theories that placed the private sphere, personal experiences, and care in opposition to the rational expression of public morality. According to these early theorists, the work to which women attended was treated as separate and lesser than the more important needs of the public. Gillens's ethic of care was tied to mothering, nurturing, and women's morality. Feminist care ethics has been rightly critiqued for forgetting this relationship between care and justice, constructing those who are disabled as "passively dependent" (Hankivsky et al., 2014, p. 254), and not properly attending to power. Tronto (1998) though, depicts care as both moral and political. Likewise Hankivsky explains,

> Care places at the forefront human flourishing and the prevention of harm and suffering. For many, care is seen as a contrast to the individual-istic nature of liberalism and a radical basis from which to rethink human nature, human needs, and how political judgments are made to ensure more democratic policies in which power is more evenly distributed.
>
> *(Hankivsky et al., 2014, p. 253)*

As Thompson (1998) points out, white feminist models of care often act in universalizing ways and rely on color-blind frameworks. These frameworks do not incorporate how Black feminist models of care are tied to a very different lived experience for Black women. Scholars have advocated for more inclusivity in the past ten years by enhancing care ethics with intersectionality (Raghuram, 2021). However, when Black women are an afterthought and Blackness is seen as simply *enhancing* the existing literature and theory, care falls short. If Black women and intersectionality are merely a mechanism to augment an already existing tool, we have missed how Black Feminist thought and Black activist and liberation work has always centered care as praxis—far before the 1970s or 1980s.

Instead, we propose that Black feminist ethics of care predate the literature in white feminist studies. Black and Africana care strategies are central to a radically intentional Black DH and require us to reconsider these origin stories, looking to the many examples of how Black communities of scholars, activists, and ordinary folks prioritize care, see care as central to justice, and integrate an ethic and praxis of care in their technical work. This chapter considers the long historical relationship between care and feeding and radical Black thought and activism. I then document institutional resistance to this practice of care in the administration of funded DH projects. Finally, I consider how this application of care and feeding moves beyond administration and human resources into the methods we use to do Black DH.

KEY QUESTIONS

- How is Black DH praxis informed by a history of care and feeding in Black activism and organizing?
- What do care and feeding look like in Black DH praxis?
- How does care in the administration of Black DH projects translate to our method?

Tracing a History of Care Strategies

Any introduction to Black DH is incomplete without attention to the Colored Conventions Project (CCP). Founded by Drs. Gabrielle Foreman, Jim Casey, and Sarah Patterson, the project started at the University of Delaware and set out to digitize the archive of deeply important, yet often overlooked, events of the Colored Conventions. The Colored Conventions were a yearly convening of Black leaders and ordinary citizens that spanned nearly seven decades. As the Colored Conventions Project outlines on their website:

> Providing a powerful structure and platform for Black organizing, more than 200 state and national Colored Conventions were held between 1830 and the 1890s. Filling churches, city hall buildings, courthouses, lecture halls, and theaters, the well-attended Colored Conventions illustrate the diversity of cultural life and political thought among Black communities and their leaders. The meetings included the most prominent writers, organizers, church leaders, newspaper editors, educators, and entrepreneurs in the canon of early African American leadership—and tens of thousands more whose names went unrecorded.
>
> *(https://coloredconventions.org/)*

CCP started in Dr. Gabrielle Foreman's graduate seminar at the University of Delaware. Project participants set out to create and enliven the record of the conventions. They have digitized, transcribed, located new records, created study guides, and provided a public forum for teachers and researchers to use the materials in various ways. The team insists on a collaborative process and community outreach. CCP has served as a model for many Black DH projects, showcasing the possibilities within the field. As a guidepost for those hoping to create their Black DH projects and providing accessibility to records now enliven online, CCP offers an oft-overlooked component of Black feminist organizing, the attention toward care and feeding.

In the 2021 edited collection, *The Colored Conventions Movement: Black Organizing in the Nineteenth Century*, Psyche Williams-Forson focuses readers' attention on the women of the movement, tracing the material culture and domestic labor that made it possible for the conventions to exist. In her essay, "Where did they eat? Where did they stay?" from which we draw the title of this chapter, Forson traces Black women's role in feeding and lodging attendees of the conventions. Forson pushes the reader to consider these questions as she examines the gaps and crevices of the archive, searching for Black women's frequent absence in the documents and pages of records from the conventions. For example, at the 1858 convention in Troy, New York, the minutes refer to "a table loaded with the most palatable refreshments, which were eaten during the recess, with a relish." This brief notation in the record does not reference who planned the menu, cooked the food, or laid out the spread. In this way, the Black women likely responsible appear to only exist in so much as those who keep the records find the product of their labor of note. As Williams-Forson (2021) explains, boarding houses, often run by Black women during the mid-1800s, were as much about an ethic of care as the financial survival of the women who ran them. Often relegated to low-paid domestic positions in major cities, Black women and men saw boarding as a mechanism to simultaneously provide care to activists traveling to their cities for the conventions and as a strategy to keep their financial wellbeing intact.

The Colored Conventions Project and Psyche Williams-Forson's research point to an intractable truth about the importance of care and feeding and the ability to locate records of such activity within our archives. CCP relies on the premise that uncovering, digitizing, and making available records of such a convention is meritorious. CCP also signals the importance of collaboration and attention to caring for records that have previously been ignored. Forson's research further argues that even within the uncovering of previously ignored records of the CCP, there remain gaps and crevices where the women live. Williams Forson's care of these records requires her to look at what is written in the available advertisements in the archive and make sense of the spaces where people live between those records. Her methods regarding material culture require attentiveness to practices of care and feeding and provide us a model for Black DH. From this example, we see that Black DH must make it our mission to think about the people that we study—and that we study *with*—as requiring our care and feeding.

The legacy of the Free Breakfast Program from the Black Panther Party likewise demonstrates how feeding is a literal mandate in recognizing the material needs of those we hope to organize and a metaphorical aim of any collaboration strategy and community. The Black Panther Party started the Free Breakfast for Children Program in 1969. At that time in this country, there was free lunch for poor children within the national school lunch program; however, breakfast programs were still limited. Bobby Seale, alongside Father O'Neill and parishioner Ruth Beckford Smith, created the program and recruited people in the neighborhood to send their children (Lateef & Androff, 2017). The Panthers took this work to more than 23 cities. Many chapters across the country enlisted the help of churches, community-based organizations, and local businesses, asking local businesses to donate items like eggs, toast, and milk. In 1969 alone, the Panthers fed more than 20,000 children nationwide. By all accounts, this was a successful way for a community organization to provide for the real and substantive material needs of the people with whom they hoped to work. The Free Breakfast for Children Program provides an example of how an organization whose aims are often thought of as being about revolution, action, policy, and politics prioritize children and their food needs as a mechanism to provide care for the community simultaneously earning trust. The Panthers, through this program, give us a way of understanding how our mandate as those responsible for graduate students and fellow faculty through the administration of our grants and DH programming must first take into account the material needs of those involved. Sometimes those needs are food-based. Other times they are based on folks' time, energy, and mental health. When we begin with food, it reminds us that we cannot focus on things like products or deliverables until people are okay. Helping folks just "be okay" must also be considered central to our work.

Psyche Williams Forson asked the vital question, "what did they eat and where did they stay?" to think through the history of the Colored Conventions. However, the Colored Conventions Project signals that care and feeding are instrumental to digitization efforts, especially when the subject/content is Black persons. Likewise, we assert that care and feeding function in two ways for those engaging in Black DH praxis. The first is as a mechanism for tracing our collaborative practice and the attentiveness to which we give the material needs of those with whom we work. The second way is about our method and approach to doing Black DH. How can we take the ideas of care and feeding and translate them to the historical archival work and online socially mediated texts that we study as a part of digital Black humanities?

History shows how care and feeding are integral to a foundational basis for radical and revolutionary organizing and activism, and the lengths institutions will go to deprioritize their implementation in our work. The Panthers' free breakfast program was a frequent target of the FBI (Bloom & Martin, 2013). Some of the mechanisms the Federal Bureau of Investigation used to destroy the program included reaching out to local stores and discouraging them from donating items, spreading rumors that food was poisoned, and even raiding sites where children were still eating their breakfast in the morning. The government understood how powerful it was to meet a community's needs right where they were. The Panthers demonstrated an ethic of care in interacting with the community. Unfortunately, the state was demonstrating itself as an armed enforcer, not of care nor community but of control. Since then, reduced and free lunch and breakfast programs have increased across the country, but only in 2021, during a global pandemic, did the United States make free breakfast and lunch accessible to all public school students. When facing a visible crisis that impacted all families and students, it seemed the federal government was willing to concede the importance of ensuring that children were well-nourished. However, this extension of understanding was again withdrawn in 2022 as the program lapsed. Well-fed, nourished children learn more. When people are not worried about their next meal, they are freer to focus, imagine, and create. So, why would a government that recognized this just one year prior remove access? As with the Panthers, the state continues to demonstrate that even when resources exist, there is little will to provide care to citizens, specifically Black and brown citizens. Doing ethical work in Black DH within an academic or research institution requires acknowledging that our organizations often act as arms of the state. Without a radically intentional praxis of care, our work often reifies these capacities of control rather than providing care and feeding to the people our work will touch.

What Do Care and Feeding Require within the Academy?

The biggest challenge to care and feeding as an intentional strategy of team building and an ethical method within Black DH is that our success metrics in the academy directly oppose what these methods produce. Early on in my directorship of AADHum, I found that the strength and vitality of our program was reliant on a community of Black and allied graduate students whose work was deeply invested in Black liberation, social justice, and Black culture. Moreover, the work that that group, our core constituency, needed was more expansive than the initial grant proposal allowed.

As a part of a program, center, or project reliant on external funding, we had obligations to our funders and university administration. These deliverables typically include partnerships with notable organizations, building new curricula, publishing books or articles, and visible programming. Further, as a tenure-track faculty member directing the program, my success metrics included traditional publications and classroom teaching. This infrastructure that asks the leaders of Black DH projects to justify their external and internal funding through traditional markers of success is decades—if not centuries old—and incredibly resistant to change. Academic culture will consistently prioritize traditional publications, traditional classrooms, and reports to funders, which contrasts with the organizing principles around community and care outlined above. Never has a grant report prompted the question: "are the people okay?"

Funding for AADHum was internal and external, and our grant leaders were also the leaders of the college. However, those tasked with daily operations of the grant, those responsible for crafting and implementing our ethical praxis, those who supervised students and staff, and those who ultimately would be responsible for the success or failure of the project were students and junior faculty who had not written the original proposal. On the one hand, having college leadership as grant PIs should alleviate some of the roadblocks that many in Black DH face regarding translating their work to their supervisors and receiving institutional support for creating sustainability in their work. However, as we found, the bureaucracies of institutions are often more potent than supportive leadership. So, at AADHum, we learned essential lessons about prioritizing care and the barriers you run into when doing so. We did not always get it right, so part of our care for you, dear reader, is writing about the successes and failures so that, hopefully, your work can exceed our own. Below I will outline two primary roadblocks to Black DH administration and some potential ways to create intentions toward care, even within these systems.

Funding and Supporting Student-Workers

Because I was transparent about my need for feeding and care specifically to keep me healthy and well, the people I worked with did just that. At the start of our working relationship, I made it clear that if I skipped meals, or if my blood sugar dipped, my personality changed and my health was in jeopardy. So, keeping a candy bar in their desks was simultaneously individual care for me and a collective commitment to the community arrangement we made at the start of our relationship: *when I am well, the team is better.*

We can translate that same sentiment to our care and commitment to the folks who work on our project teams. I believe in starting with arrangements or agreements at the start of our labor relationships with one another. When a new student or associate is hired on the team, it is crucial to determine what they need to get out of this project in the most honest and transparent way possible. Each team member, regardless of rank, must have the comfort and the ease to be clear about what they bring to the team and what they expect in return. This is especially crucial when caring for precarious student workers and staff who may simply need money or course credit. While it is possible to love your work, what we are ultimately asking of students, specifically Black students on Black DH projects, is for their labor. They have every right to, in turn, ask for fair compensation for that labor. There may be other cases where they need to learn better strategies for writing. They may need a publication. Writing, even in small amounts, as part of a project team can help students who carry anxiety about their place in the academy. Other folks joining our teams need to acquire a specific skill set. Suppose a graduate student needs to learn a programming language and sees your project as a means to that end. Is there really any problem with that as long as they are willing to work within the parameters and ethics you have established for your project? Allowing them to oversee portions of the project where they lack confidence may ultimately allow them to do that same work outside the project to meet their goals of publication or graduation. All these needs are sometimes intertwined but are all, on their own, valid reasons for accepting the labor of doing Black DH. However, along the way, it can become very easy for the needs of the project to take over the needs of the individual.

So to develop a dialectic of self and community (Steele, 2021), leadership has to take on the role of care and feeding to ensure that when someone's blood sugar drops, there is a candy bar present. Or when their writing lags, there is a writing project present. The assignment of tasks cannot simply be about who is best equipped to handle them. It also has to be about who needs this task and how this task advances what they hope to accomplish. Ultimately, Black DH labs and centers can and must reconcile the dual nature of student lives as learners and laborers, and serve as an example to the rest of the university.

Our system of pay for graduate students is abysmal nationwide. Many of our students live in precarity. Graduate education was once reserved for those whose familial and financial circumstances allowed for prolonged study without worry about money. While the system still favors those of higher economic status through testing, admissions, social networking, and institutional prestige, we have long since opened higher education to those across the financial spectrum. However, our system of graduate assistantships and stipends does not match our time. The minimal stipends graduate students receive regularly situate them in poverty during their time in school. This is especially true for Black and Brown students, first-generation students, children of immigrants, victims of familial abuse, and generally those without a parental safety net. For those who use graduate student labor in our digital projects, this reality should impact how we think about funding, labor, and training. How can we provide care within a system where labor is undervalued, the university sets wages, and graduate students live in precarity?

When writing out the grant budget, we should be aware of the university systems that often limit student labor, and ask students about the mechanisms they have already found to elude those systems. For example, international students are often only allowed to work a certain number of hours based on the terms of their visas. If your budget only allows hourly work or overloads from graduate students, you may be excluding them before they have had the chance to apply. For other students, overloads or extra hourly pay can be desirable ways to earn income beyond the hours of their regular assistantship. Therefore, only allocating full-time assistantships in your budget precludes the appointment of students who need to retain their departmental assistantship while taking on extra labor via overloads or hourly pay. Building flexibility into the grant budget allows you to have the broadest possible pool for hiring. It also requires you to design and advocate for flexible positions. Developing the language to explain this phenomenon to university administration and external funders is part of the work of caring for your future hires. This flexibility may translate to using two students for work you initially imagined as appropriate for one. It may also mean considering how to stretch your project via no-cost extensions into the summer so that students unable to work extra hours during the academic year can join the team and contribute in valuable ways while earning extra income beyond the traditional boundaries of the academic calendar. Faculty may often be far removed from their years in graduate school and/or unfamiliar with the specific funding structures where they teach and research. However, as project directors or PIs (Principal Investigators) on grants, this is not a task that should be outsourced to another administrator in the business or finance office. How we materially care for our project team is a central and core guiding principle for ethical DH work.

When planning the *Intentionally Digital, Intentionally Black* conference, our team had three graduate students: one full-time, one half-time, and one hourly. In full transparency, those students worked more hours than they should have for weeks. Some work happened at home, some required evening commitments, and some put off projects and responsibilities in other parts of their lives to contribute to the success of that conference. While it was a tremendous learning experience for conference planning, budgeting, marketing, and general campus administration, I had to be honest that their learning was not my primary focus during that window of time. As often as possible, we tried at AADHum to create task lists and labor that were mutually beneficial. For example, if you studied and worked on social media, perhaps you are best equipped to run social media accounts. If you need more experience in teaching, perhaps you could plan and host learning sessions focusing on the tools or theory you need to practice for your own research. Nevertheless, at conference planning time, it was all-hands-on-deck. During this period, I remember sending a student home one evening and refusing to tell them that I was staying later to finish, as they had already put in far more than their required 20 hours that week. However, this was an exception, rather than the rule it should have been. It is a fact that the work of academics often comes in fits and starts. When finishing a project, you sometimes write, build, and code for hours. In contrast, other weeks are a light reading load and perhaps attending a few workshops. After managing our way through those long and challenging weeks and months, we learned that we had to build those lulls into our practice of care rather than expecting them to come naturally.

We did so by drafting plans for our time that we shared openly with one another (see Figure 3.1). We wanted to let each other know when this project would not be our priority. We wanted to be honest about when other life things could and should take precedence. So, we developed a work chart—ever-changing though it may have been.

Much of the intentionality described above should apply across the university; however, we contend that doing Black DH requires specific attention to this care work as part of a larger political project at the intersection of digital research and Black studies. Building in time for care does not always look like providing food and laughter over a meal. Instead, care may be providing paid space and time away from the project. When overloaded with work from other projects, classes, and research, our students often took breaks from team meetings and the regular weekly tasks they were assigned. As a student, it can be challenging to advocate for these breaks, so it is incumbent upon those in authority to not only make these suggestions but to model this kind of care for ourselves. Unfortunately, Audre Lorde's words on self-care have frequently become commodified in an era on "self-care" strategies as outlined by online influencers and BuzzFeed listicles. Inna Michaeli warns against this neo-liberal co-option of self-care by insisting that care as theorized by Lorde must not be the private responsibility of the individual, nor should care "obscure[e] the social, economic and political sources of physical, emotional, and spiritual distress and exhaustion, or be depoliticized" (Michaeli, 2017, p. 52). I stepped away from AADHum as director for short periods to write, recharge, and attend to personal family issues. I also took an entire semester of leave to work on my book manuscript. During this time, through the praxis of care we cultivated as a team, I could fully trust that the

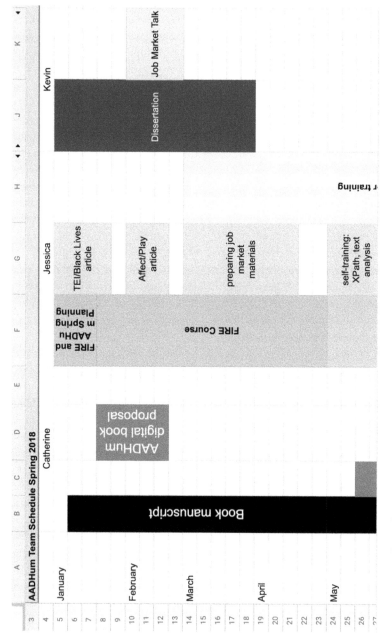

FIGURE 3.1 Author's shared work chart from 2019.

project would move forward without my physical presence. After the AADHum conference, our team required weeks of individual and collective recuperation. We built in the lulls, ensuring that students who put in the extra time leading up to the conference were fairly compensated for that work. We modeled care for self as a necessary part of team building, DH project planning, and a future strategy for their careers in academia.

Creating Black-Centric, Not Tool-Centric, Programming

Designing programming for our community is another avenue where we led with care and feeding and further attempted to avoid the barriers of institutional resistance to this model. AADHum was fortunate to develop at an institution with a long-standing relationship with DH. With one of the oldest DH institutes in the country as our founding partner, we had little to worry about in terms of having the staff and infrastructure to offer training on digital tools. However, we saw our task as cultivating a different kind of space. We imagined and designed an environment where people were prioritized over tools—rather than the more common DH space where folks show up, learn a tool, and take their knowledge back only to their own individual project. Our approach required those who wished to study histories or cultures of Blackness to connect socially, intellectually, and emotionally with Black persons and communities. We achieved this goal through creating learning spaces that required readings outside of DH, and focused on Black thought, theory, and history. We forged an expectation that those with the knowledge of tools and techniques could not simply show up to teach, but were also required to recognize the expertise of Black thinkers outside of digital studies. Our programming fed a need in DH—that those who would build careers on examining the diasporic histories of Blackness would not treat Black culture as a site of research but as a revered space to which they could and should prove worthy of welcome.

This decentering of tools is counter to the rationale used by many in applying for funding in the DH. What intrigues many funders and university administrators is the extent to which DH might be reinvigorating the humanities writ large, which continues to struggle with low enrollment and unending stories in the popular press about the death of humanistic inquiry. Digital tools excite undergraduates and give many administrators the flashy products and projects that can be used to sell skeptical parents on degrees in literature and history. DH are also one of the few places in humanistic inquiry to secure significant grant funding from private and governmental agencies. However, Black DH must pivot from this model if it hopes to remain true to Black studies as a field.

As Crouchett (1971) explains, "at the turn of the century, a Black studies' curriculum was simply a course in Negro history" (p. 195). Yet in the late 1960s, led by a decentralized network of student activists across the nation, The Black Studies Movement was born. Bunzel quoting Nathan Hare, Special Coordinator of Black Studies at San Francisco State in 1968, writes, the whole idea of Black

Studies is "more far-reaching than appears on the surface." His conversations with academicians across the country on the education of Black Americans leave no doubt in his mind that even those who have accepted the idea of Black Studies do not fully understand its need. "They see the goal as the mere Blackening of white courses, in varying number and degree," he writes. "They omit in their program the key component of community involvement and collective stimulation." Their program is individualistic, aimed at "rehabilitating" individual students by means of pride in culture, racial contributions generally, and regenerated dignity and self-esteem. "They fail to see that the springboard for all of this is an animated communalism aimed at a Black educational renaissance." Thus many well-intentioned efforts, Hare says, are doomed to inevitable failure. "They comprise piecemeal programs that, being imported, are based on an external perspective." Put simply, they are white, not Black (Bunzel, 1968, p. 29). Suppose Black DH is simply DH with Black subjects. In that case, this sub-field will follow on a path that abdicates the goals of liberation in favor of centering projects that produce capital investment—without investment in Black people and Black liberation. As funding for Black DH increases, it is incumbent upon those writing the grants and those reading them to locate principles that do not assume digital tools are more vital to Black DH than Black theory, thought, and persons.

While we intentionally removed tools from the center of DH, we were not naive about the importance that introductions to new tools could have for Black studies scholars from various disciplines. Indeed part of our work was ensuring students and faculty access to the tools they would need to advance their work. We advocated for the university to buy licenses for the tools that would advance the work of graduate students and partnered with colleges across the university to ensure access. Even as this was incredibly beneficial to the campus community, we pushed back against tool-based programming that assumed a lack of expertise on the part of Black faculty and students that can only be remedied through instruction from outsiders.

KEY LESSONS: BLACK DH PRAXIS OF CARE

Black DH praxis of care requires flexibility within the inflexibility of the system that was not designed to liberate and provide support Black person.

Black DH praxis of care foregrounds feeding our community by prioritizing the material needs of students and precarious faculty and staff when developing programming and allocating resources.

Black DH praxis of care relies on our own knowledge, expertise, resources, and labor as scholars and practitioners already marginalized within the academy and DH.

Black DH praxis of care means decentering tools in favor of affirming Black theory, experiences, and cultural practices of learning, doing, and making.

Matching Our Methods to Our Values

Thus far we have considered what it means to place care at the center of DH projects and grant administration: centralizing the needs of the people with whom we work and designating those practices as foundational necessities, not add-ons, to doing the work of Black DH. But what of the Black DH projects themselves? We propose that care and feeding likewise translate to our methods and tools in Black DH.

Black DH often requires researchers to work across types of texts, and with different genres of materials that were produced and created in entirely different ways using different tools, and sometimes in different centuries. Some digital scholars of Black studies look toward the past, centralizing their work in the archive. They dig through crates and records. They digitize documents of slaveholdings, freedom papers, memoirs, and correspondence that undergird our understanding of Black life in the 18th or 19th centuries. Other Black DH scholars locate their work online and in socially mediated spaces like Twitter, Instagram, or TikTok. For far too long, these scholars have seen their work as separate, rarely considering the other to be a part of the DH. But as discussed in Chapter 2, Black DH has forced a conversation between historians, media scholars, and sociologists. When Black thought, Black theory, and Black persons are at the center of our research, it becomes less important to maintain strict allegiances to the disciplinary homes from which we draw our inquiry and more important to remain committed to Black folks. So, how do we begin to develop ethical practices in Black DH, given that scholars who claimed this mantle do and will continue to exist in different disciplines, with very different methods and corpora of study? How do archival work and online data collection marry—or, to raise a more specific hypothetical, can and should we apply similar strategies when dealing with correspondence written in 1898 *and* a tweet sent in 2019?

We contend that considerations of care traverse Black DH praxis, involving computational methods, deep readings of digitized texts from the 19th century, and analysis of tweets and hashtags. Any strategy or method for studying Black history and culture with digital tools, or within a digital culture, must situate the texts historically and contextually and focus on the people that use the tools— rather than just the tools themselves. Ultimately, Black DH ask us to think about the relationship that folks form with their tools. How can we care for the people whose words, documents, and life stories we find in the archive? How might we see the tweets and posts from social media users as part of their life stories, rather than detached diatribes shouted into the ether? How can our technical skills and innovations be leveraged to discover novel ways of caring for those who contribute their words, artifacts, and experiences to our work? Put simply: we can choose to be present, to extend care, and to feed, metaphorically, the people whose work and words we touch with our research.

So what does a radically intentional method look like in Black DH? I was fortunate to begin work in earnest on my first book project, *Digital Black Feminism*, while directing the AADHum initiative. My book project, born of my experience with care and feeding at AADHum, traces the long relationship between Black women and technology, beginning in the antebellum south and traversing the social media landscape of Twitter and Instagram. This task drew together disparate corners of Black DH praxis, requiring archival work on documents from the 18th and 19th centuries, born-digital archiving and text analysis of blogs from 10–15 years prior, and digital ethnographic work on fleeting posts like Instagram stories. While giving talks on the book, I regularly remark how it would not exist but for the opportunity to spend time with archivists, historians, librarians, sociologists, and computer scientists gathering together in the same space and forcing a reconciliation of aims and methods. There are two lessons on method from *Digital Black Feminism* that demonstrate the praxis of care in Black DH projects.

So many folks in Black DH work with historical materials and rely heavily on the care provided by archivists in managing fonds of material to the series, file, and item level. New digital projects emerge from their work and the research guides they create. To study Black feminist technoculture in *Digital Black Feminism*, I relied on the existing archival material for three Black women writers in the 20th and 21st centuries. Their materials spanned categories like diaries, correspondence, and speeches. I am grateful to the archivists who took pages and pages of material and created categories that provided me guidance about the context in which each was created. For example, Ida B. Wells, writing in her Memphis diary, took a different approach to her prose than she would in *The Red Record*. The archivist's work to sort and provide structure to the archive allows researchers to decide what is worthy of study and how to proceed. We can simultaneously hold gratitude for this skill and labor while reflecting on how our own praxis of care may differ from those charged with keeping, managing, and sorting those documents. In defining and making a case for critical archival studies, Caswell, Punzalan, and Sangwand (2017) explain that archives have the power to shape "fundamental humanities assumptions about how we exist in the world, how we know what we know, and how we transmit that knowledge"(p. 4). Archives historically have inadequately served the immediate needs of marginalized publics (Gilliland, 2017), failed to document the long history of violence against Black communities (Sutherland, 2017), and instead should disrupt locations of power and agency (Kelleher, 2017).

For those working with historical records in Black DH, we must carefully consider how the selection of materials and the categorization of documents can lead to erasure and harm to Black people. As Sharpe explains, "Again and again scholars of slavery face absences in the archives as we attempt to find 'the agents buried beneath' (Spillers, 2003), the accumulated erasures, projections, fabulations, and misnamings" (Sharpe, 2016, p. 12). We must take care not to replicate this pattern, instead seeing the humanity in Black folks whose names, documents, and lives we situate at the center of our work. Sharpe goes on,

> We are expected to discard, discount, disregard, jettison, abandon, and measure those ways of knowing and enact epistemic violence that we know to be violence against others and ourselves. In other words, for Black academics to produce legible work in the academy often means adhering to research methods that are "drafted into the service of a larger destructive force" (Saunders, 2008, p. 67), thereby doing violence to our capacities to read, think, and imagine otherwise. Despite knowing otherwise, we are often disciplined into thinking through and along lines that reinscribe our own annihilation, reinforcing and reproducing what Sylvia Wynter has called our "narratively condemned status" (Wynter, 2018, p. 70).
>
> *(Sharpe, 2016, p. 13)*

Instead, as Williams-Forson's work on the Colored Conventions project reminds us, we must be attentive to the gaps—the places where Black people, especially Black women, are not a part of the record. For example, Black women's labor, expertise, and technological skill are often removed from our records because Black women were not permitted to keep or maintain those records. Therefore Black DH projects that purport to care for Black people must privilege the lived experience of Black people and non-binary folks. We must, as Sharpe contends,

> become undisciplined. The work we do requires new modes and methods of research and teaching; "new ways of entering and leaving the archives of slavery, of undoing the racial calculus and … political arithmetic that were entrenched centuries ago" (Hartman, 2008, p. 6) and that live into the present.
>
> *(Sharpe, 2016, p. 13)*

We can develop alternate means of sorting and sifting in the archive, bringing light to previously unkept spaces and recontextualizing the records to better illuminate the fullness of Black folks in our history and future.

From these sorting and sifting strategies, we take lessons for how we approach contemporary born-digital texts. Blogs, Instagram posts, and tweets already use a system of categorization based on metadata. The initial mechanism we have for sorting is done through tags, hashtags, or other means separate from the researcher, developed by the users or the affordance of the platform (for example, location data attached to tweets or hashtags used by TikTok content creators). However, none of these are sufficient on their own to understand and document the full context of the work. For example, an online writer may document the same event using the same hashtag across platforms. However, our task as researchers is to know how each platform's imagined affordances (Nagy & Neff, 2015) take root in that author's choices and further how even the use of the same hashtag might serve different purposes across the sites. Typically, it is impossible to grasp this by only looking into their use of one platform at one moment. In the same way that we advocate for an administrative practice that takes into account the fullness of the individual team members, I likewise insist that our method for studying the digital products of Black folks and using tools to study the artifacts of Black culture require care and attentiveness to the content creator/author's work over time and across contexts.

Those in Black DH must develop a relationship with slow work when the subject of their digital scholarship are Black people. This is not to say that big data projects and computational analysis should be avoided in favor of only close readings. Instead, we are advocating for slow work as a praxis of care for texts, researchers, and readers. Moya Bailey makes the strong case that DH scholarship that hopes to engage the lives and liberation of Black people must slow down. Bailey argues for moving at the "pace of trust." She explains,

> An ethics of pace means that the ends do not justify the means but, rather, that the means are the ends. By remaining attentive to the people involved in our research, keeping the human at the center of DH, we can create a process that does not cause harm, or at least reduces it. The pace of life and the pace of our research are something humans can control.
>
> *(Bailey, 2021, p. 295)*

As Berger argues, slowness brings "more time spent with the projects and more meaningful relationships with the topic(s)" (Berger, 2019). Care as Black DH method and praxis informs the *how* of our research and the choice in what subject and content material is appropriate for inquiry within Black DH.

As outlined earlier in this text, what constitutes Black DH research is still being determined. For many years, humanistic research using digital tools as the primary definition of DH led to a heavy emphasis on historical and literature-based DH research. For some, this meant that any project whose subject or content area was Black people or culture would be considered Black DH. While some of our most innovative digital projects belong to this category, so too do projects done by those with no commitments to Black persons, our history, or our culture. Any scholar who did a project on enslavement, African American art, or James Baldwin while using Voyant, ArcGIS, or text encoding may see their work as contributing to Black DH research. Care may not have been a consideration, but it must be moving forward.

In Black DH, our "topic" is the lived experience and/or cultural artifacts of Black folks whose lives are far too often met with state and systemic violence and exploitation from researchers, journalists, politicians, and curators.

Therefore, radically intentional care as a method in Black DH fights not only against the exploitative nature of an academic system that pushes a publish-or-perish mantra but also against DH projects that violently exploit Black communities with little to no regard for what is left in the wake. Christina Sharpe reminds us that Blackness is lived in the wake. However, as she concludes,

> If we are lucky, we live in the knowledge that the wake has positioned us as no-citizen. If we are lucky, the knowledge of this positioning avails us particular ways of re/seeing, re/inhabiting, and re/imagining the world. And we might use these ways of being in the wake in our responses to terror and the varied and various ways that our Black lives are lived under occupation.

In their pioneering issue of *The Black Scholar*, Jessica Maria Johnson and Marc Anthony Neal provide just such a response with Black Code Studies.

Black Code Studies as described by Johnson and Neal (2017) fiercely advocate for research that "refutes conceptions of the digital that remove Black diasporic people from engagement with technology, modernity, or the future. It centers Black thought and cultural production across a range of digital platforms." They go on to explain,

> It is the viral Blackness that, described by Wade, "subverts social hierarchies by putting the needs and desires of Black bodies at the center." It is the #Blktwitterstorians hashtag, created by Brown and Crutchfield to highlight Black historians and history. It is Blackness as a deep humanism and affect(ion) that confronts, as Driscoll shows, the biopolitics of the hexadecimal, and, as Greene-Hayes and James discuss, the biopolitics of organizing and everyday anti-Blackness.
>
> *(Johnson & Neal, 2017, p. 2)*

The similar throughline in each of the works they name is the organizing principle from these authors, activists, and artists around deep and profound care for Black folks. Care, in our research and methods within Black DH, requires a commitment that lasts longer than most external funds or institutional whims, and certainly longer than the tenure of any administrator with authority to green-light or pull the plug on a project. Black DH, therefore, requires the administration of care for the Black people, texts, thoughts, ideas, and spaces that we study, create within, and build alongside. Care as praxis and ethics would therefore undermine any singular project by a scholar whose commitments to productivity or promotion supersede their commitment to Blackness.

FUNDAMENTAL PRINCIPLES OF BLACK DIGITAL HUMANITIES METHODS

Care for texts, data, and participants. While our approach to Black Digital Studies may differ greatly based on our discipline, there are in fact strategies of care that traverse these boundaries. We can take principles from archival work and apply them to data gathered from social media. We can treat participants in qualitative work as whole humans who bring unique vantage points to our work and then extend this practice to how we treat the words of folks in places like Twitter or Instagram. Our care praxis must move beyond method.

Care for the persons whose lives are impacted by our work. Thinking beyond institutional guidelines, we can forge relationships of care with the communities we draw knowledge from and that we produce knowledge for.

Slow work and an ethic of care. When our study turns to Black persons and the artifacts of Black culture, we often need to slow down to build the kind of context needed to approach this work with care and context.

Situate work historically and contextually to deprioritize tools. Even as we recognize the importance of digital tools in opening new lines of inquiry and making possible collaborative projects that may not have existed just years ago, we emphasize the importance of deprioritizing tools in Black DH. We urge practitioners to think carefully about how focus on objects can inadvertently draw attention away from people. Ultimately we want to make sure that just because we *can* do a project, that we *should*.

Radical Reflections for Care-Centered Collaborative Research

For each of us, commitment to care and feeding began before we joined the team but was fortified as central to our values in building AADHum. For example, my parents instilled in me the idea that for whatever reasons someone visited your home, they should not leave hungry. It was my responsibility to feed them. In academia, we are rushed through programs, encouraged to publish quickly, and often provided few resources to do the teaching and service work. Likewise, scholars of digital studies often chase the newest technology, creating tools for faster analysis of more data and more efficient means of digitizing and archiving records. Yet those interested in centering Black theory and Black persons in our digital scholarship are a part of a lineage that requires us to ensure our labor feeds our community and that our students do not go hungry, both materially and intellectually. Material support for our teams requires grant administrators to shift priorities in a time when we are dependent on outcomes to satisfy external stakeholders and funders. Even as humanities funding becomes reliant on external support, there are yet mechanisms within institutions to resist external metrics that prevent the slow work, care, and feeding that makes for healthier humans doing the work and, in turn, better and more ethical work products.

I began this chapter by reminiscing about the food we shared as a team. Every time I make ramen at home, I still think about those shared meals. I recognize that in feeding each other, we created a radically intentional praxis of care that helped feed a lot of other folks in Black DH. Lisa Bass links Black feminist ethics of care in educational leadership to an ethic of risk. As she explains, care requires

> respond[ing] to injustices within the educational system often without considering the consequences; even when it involves placing [ourselves] at risk. This expression of caring is an example of the ethic of risk, which encompasses identifying with the cause, being responsible to take action, and being willing to accept the consequences.
>
> *(Bass, 2012, p. 84)*

The willingness to put our reputation or projects at risk to remain steadfast in our extensions of care to our team, collaborators, texts, and data is no small ask. However, if Black DH research is to make inroads in feeding and caring for Black folks, it must be a risk worth taking.

RADICAL REFLECTIONS FOR BLACK DH LAB/CENTER LEADERS

- How can I provide a space that feeds my team?
- How can care guide this project toward aims more aligned with Black liberation?
- What do my hiring, advising and mentoring practices suggest about my relationship with a Black praxis of care?
- What are the unique programmatic needs of the community of scholars that I wish to support with this project?
- How am I promoting methods for learners that center care?
- How can I serve as a resource for precarious staff, faculty and students attached to this Black DH project?
- How can I match my ethics to the promises made to funders and/or university administration?
- Are there others better/more equipped to provide training in either DH tools or Black studies that I should consider as partners in this work?

References

Bailey, M. (2021). The ethics of pace. *South Atlantic Quarterly, 120*(2), 285–299. https://doi.org/10.1215/00382876-8916032

Bass, L. (2012). When care trumps justice: The operationalization of Black feminist caring in educational leadership. *International Journal of Qualitative Studies in Education, 25*(1), 73–87. https://doi.org/10.1080/09518398.2011.647721

Berger, C. (2019). The importance of reflection: A call for slow digital humanities. *Digital.*

Bloom, J., & Martin, W. E. (2013). *Black against Empire: The History and Politics of the Black.* University of California Press.

Bunzel, J. H. (1968). Black Studies at San Francisco State. *The Public Interest, 13,* 22–38.

Caswell, M., Punzalan, R., & Sangwand, T.-K. (2017). Critical archival studies: An introduction. *Journal of Critical Library and Information Studies, 1*(2).

Crouchett, L. (1971). Early black studies movements. *Journal of Black Studies, 2*(2), 189–200.

Frontiers Annual Conference. (2019). Austin, Texas, United States. https://digital.library.txstate.edu/handle/10877/9487

Gilligan, C. (1977). In a different voice: Women's conceptions of self and of morality. *Harvard Educational Review, 47*(4), 481–517.

Gilliland, A. J. (2017). A matter of life or death: A critical examination of the role of records and archives in supporting the agency of the forcibly displaced. *Journal of Critical Library and Information Studies, 1*(2), Article 2. https://doi.org/10.24242/jclis.v1i2.36

Hartman, S. (2008). Venus in two acts. *Small Axe: A Caribbean Journal of Criticism, 12*(2), 1–14.

Hankivsky, O., Grace, D., Hunting, G., Giesbrecht, M., Fridkin, A., Rudrum, S., … & Clark, N. (2014). An intersectionality-based policy analysis framework: critical reflections on a methodology for advancing equity. *International Journal for Equity in Health, 13*(1), 1–16.

Johnson, J. M., & Neal, M. A. (2017). Introduction: Wild seed in the machine. *The Black Scholar, 47*(3), 1–2.

Kelleher, C. (2017). Archives without archives: (Re)Locating and (Re)Defining the archive through post-custodial praxis. *Journal of Critical Library and Information Studies, 1*(2), Article 2. https://doi.org/10.24242/jclis.v1i2.29

Lateef, H., & Androff, D. (2017). Children can't learn on an empty stomach: The black panther party's free breakfast program. *Journal of Sociology & Social Welfare, 44*(4), 3–18.

Michaeli, I. (2017). Self-care: An act of political warfare or a neoliberal trap? *Development, 60*(1), 50–56.

Nagy, P., & Neff, G. (2015). Imagined affordance: Reconstructing a keyword for communication theory. *Social Media+ Society, 1*(2), 2056305115603385.

Panther Party (n.d.) (1st ed.). University of California Press. www.jstor.org/stable/10.1525/j.ctt1ppvd4

Raghuram, P. (2021). Race and feminist care ethics: Intersectionality as method. In Hoda Mahmoudi, Alison Brysk, and Kate Seaman (Eds.), *The Changing Ethos of Human Rights.* Edward Elgar Publishing.

Saunders, P. (2008). Defending the dead, confronting the archive: A conversation with M. NourbeSe Philip. *Small Axe, 12*(2), 63–79.

Sharpe, C. E. (2016). *In the wake: On blackness and being* (Vol. 1–1 online resource (xi, 175 pages): illustrations). Duke University Press. www.dawsonera.com/depp/reader/protected/external/AbstractView/S9780822373452

Spillers, H. J. (2003). *Black, white, and in color: Essays on American literature and culture.* University of Chicago Press.

Steele, C. K. (2021). *Digital black feminism.* New York University Press.

Sutherland, T. (2017). Archival amnesty: In search of black american transitional and restorative justice. *Journal of Critical Library and Information Studies, 2.*

Thompson, A. (1998). Not the color purple: Black feminist lessons for educational caring. *Harvard Educational Review, 68*(4), 522–555.

Tronto, J. C. (1998). An ethic of care. *Generations: Journal of the American Society on Aging, 22*(3), 15–20.

Williams-Forson, P. (2021). Where did they eat? Where did they stay? Interpreting material culture of black women's domesticity in the context of the colored conventions. In S. L. Patterson, P. G. Foreman, & J. Casey (Eds.), *The colored conventions movement: Black organizing in the nineteenth century.* UNC Press Books.

Wynter, S. (2018). *No humans involved.* Publication Studio Hudson.

4

IF YOU TEACH IT, THEY WILL COME

Developing Pedagogy for Black DH

Jessica H. Lu

The most rewarding days of the African American History, Culture, and Digital Humanities Initiative (AADHum) were also the most exhausting. After nearly three full years of experimental programming, the AADHum initiative culminated with its national conference, organized around the theme "intentionally digital, intentionally Black." It was an opportunity to convene a burgeoning Black digital humanities (DH) community that included over 300 scholars from across the U.S., Europe, and the Caribbean. Much of the conference's agenda highlighted major themes, questions, and methods shaping Black DH research. In many ways, the conference also captured AADHum's value in the community, as a mechanism of resource-sharing and a facilitator of intellectual and social connection among scholars scattered across the globe.

Throughout that weekend, I juggled multiple roles—I checked that rooms were equipped with enough tables and chairs, I helped troubleshoot unexpected technical issues, I shook hands and helped with hosting duties, and more. My most important job, though, was to finally shine a much-needed spotlight on one key AADHum enterprise that had, up until that point, received relatively scant attention. Among the many panels and presentations during the conference, just one roundtable discussion was intentionally aimed toward questions of pedagogy.

The roundtable, entitled "FIRE and Freedom: Bringing AADHum into the Undergraduate Classroom," offered an opportunity for Black DH communities to learn about a course called "Digital Archives," AADHum's singular entry point into undergraduate education. As the instructor for the course, I served as moderator for the conference roundtable, but it was the students who taught the lesson that day. Sophia Crooks, Kayla Graham, Ariana Lawson, Alice Liu, and

DOI: 10.4324/9781003299134-5

Courtney Richardson—all University of Maryland sophomores, and all women of color—addressed a full conference room of scholars, faculty, and administrators, as well as a live-streaming audience.

In the hours prior to the roundtable, we took photos together in the lobby of the conference venue, the Samuel Riggs IV Alumni Center, while their parents and family members looked on with pride. It was a momentous occasion for each of them; it was their first—perhaps only—appearance at a national academic conference. I remember feeling excited and nervous, sharing in their presentation jitters as though it was my first conference, too. In some ways, it was. Never before had I presented alongside undergraduate students, and never before did I feel like the stakes of a roundtable discussion were quite so high. As I looked upon their uneasy smiles, I felt proud of them and their willingness to enter this new intellectual and social terrain. Whether they realized it in that moment or not, their presence demanded attention to the proverbial elephant in the room: while junior and established scholars still struggle to carve out and hold space for Black DH work, what energy remains to invest in the next generation of Black DH scholars?

It was this one roundtable among many that arguably captured an underappreciated keystone of the AADHum initiative: teaching. From my vantage point, the greatest, fundamental challenge of AADHum's work—in scholarly training, institutional modeling, and undergraduate education—was a pedagogical one. In this chapter, I hope to share what we learned about the development of pedagogical ethics and practices in Black DH and their relationship to the overall development of the field and its future, by drawing especially on AADHum's efforts in undergraduate education. In doing so, I propose several fundamental principles of radically intentional pedagogy in Black DH and present for consideration a series of purposeful reflections for Black DH teachers.

KEY QUESTIONS

- What pedagogical practices guide our efforts to invest in the next generation of Black DH scholars?
- What is Black DH pedagogy?
- What questions and assumptions ground a Black DH classroom?
- How does radical intentionality shape practices of teaching, learning, and assessment in Black DH?

"Digital Archives" for Undergraduate Education

AADHum was designed to bring together African Americanist scholars to reimagine their research and scholarship through DH tools, methods, and techniques, and further envision, design, and test various models for Black DH initiatives. As discussed in earlier chapters, AADHum's programming piloted a series of workshops and critical discussions to teach digital skills grounded in rich understandings of Black cultural practices, theory, and history. This, too, was pedagogy, but these programs were explicitly targeted toward graduate students and faculty, with the implicit assumption that teaching the teachers would plant the necessary seeds for Black DH to grow fuller, healthier, and expansively throughout the university—and perhaps, one day, the academy. We also endeavored to experiment with different forms of programming in the hopes of one day being able to teach others how to do this work of building Black DH initiatives and communities in other institutions and contexts. These efforts consumed most of our time and energy—but we had to find a bit more to fulfill another ask in the initial grant proposal.

The initiative's singular entry point into undergraduate education was to be facilitated in partnership with the University of Maryland's First-Year Innovation and Research Experience (FIRE) program. FIRE is a three-semester program that invites first-year undergraduates to contribute directly to faculty research, overwhelmingly STEM-focused in both inquiry and method. In stark contrast to the large lectures typical of a student's first year, the FIRE program provides students with opportunities to be mentored one-on-one by faculty, work autonomously in hands-on lab settings, and explore the possibilities of producing their own scholarly research.[1]

It was not until the end of my first full year working with AADHum, when I was preparing to defend my dissertation and about to be promoted to Postdoctoral Associate, when I learned about AADHum's partnership with FIRE. As a new Postdoctoral Associate, I was to be charged with conceiving of an undergraduate course—or "research stream"—to contribute to the FIRE curriculum. I was thrilled to be focusing some of my energy on undergraduate teaching, where I have always felt most at home in the academy, but the weight of the task felt daunting. First, I was acutely aware that this course would be challenging to teach in such a way that both equipped first-year students with research skills and empowered them as knowledge-makers in the world. Second, I was also informed that my course would be the first humanities research opportunity for the first-year students in the STEM-dominated FIRE program, and I felt pressure to prove that humanities research—my methods of critical-historical textual analysis, in particular—was just as rigorous and valuable as scientific and quantitative inquiry. Third, I knew that the course would be AADHum's only focused effort to reach undergraduate students and engage in purposeful pedagogical self-study. It was a chance for us to imagine how Black DH translates to an undergraduate classroom, and how we might extend the work of Black DH community-building into an environment that was wholly unfamiliar with Black DH, its vocabularies, and the institutional matrices of power that shape the field. What course could I possibly conceive that might satisfy all three wishes?

In January 2018, I launched my course, "Digital Archives."[2] Its design was first informed by the imperatives of AADHum's mission applied to undergraduate pedagogy: to introduce first-year students to fundamental concepts, methods, and theories of Black DH research through hands-on learning. It was further shaped by my own research. At the time, I was dreaming of extending my dissertation, which focused on the rhetorical history of *freedom* as an idea, constituted by language, in Black history and culture. I was eager to supplement my training in traditional methods of rhetorical criticism with digital ones—namely, the use of extensible markup language, especially the Text Encoding Initiative (TEI) standard.[3] I was eager to move beyond textual analysis toward collecting, analyzing, and digitally modeling Black discourse that grapples with the question, *what does it mean to be free?*

"Digital Archives" was therefore conceived as a course that would allow students, too, to explore their own notions of Black freedom, as they saw it being defined, enacted, lived, and pursued in their own worlds. The course was also a vehicle through which students could produce research of their own, whether by contributing to a publishable manuscript or public-facing digital material (e.g. a web archive or crowd-sourced corpus of scholarly editions) that could provide for deeper analysis of Black freedom texts. With archives as the central organizing principle of the course, I grounded students in the same scholarly literature that propelled my own research forward: collections (both digital and non-digital) as white supremacist sites of power (Caswell, 2017); digital technologies as tools for racial justice as well as racist oppression (Browne, 2015; Gallon, 2016; Noble, 2018); and scholarly editions as born- and living- digital monuments to Black resistance and rhetorical innovation.

The students were tasked with investigating their own digital worlds and curating a collection of texts (essays, social media posts, images, videos, etc.) that engaged Black freedom in any way that piqued their interest. Their final research assignment was to use TEI markup to encode their collections, creating scholarly editions. The focus, however, was not mastering TEI. Instead, our shared goal was to create something resembling—or aspiring toward—liberatory archives (Drake, 2016). We endeavored to create digital corpora that not only modeled the original texts but further embedded critical interpretation, analysis, and context that underscored the nuances and imperatives of Black freedom in contemporary America.

Two students, Courtney Richardson and Ariana Lawson, paired up to encode texts that affirmed Black women's natural hair styling and maintenance as a defiant expression of Black women's bodily freedom in a culture dominated by violent, hegemonic standards of white beauty. Another pair of students, Sophia Crooks and Kayla Graham, took note of the overwhelming response to the 2018 Marvel film *Black Panther* and worked together to identify, study, and encode Black users' online discussions of the film, focusing on how it speculated a free society that celebrated the excellence, technological prowess, and cultural markers of the Black diaspora. Another student, Alice Liu, chose to use text encoding to explore how Black musical artists like J. Cole and Beyoncé leverage their online platforms to condemn police brutality in the United States.

While the students' respective foci diverged, their collaborative work allowed them to think broadly about the power and pitfalls of collecting, appraising, encoding, and modeling Black textual materials for digital preservation and study. At the same time, we were together learning what it meant—and how it felt—to be in a Black DH classroom. As I led the "Digital Archives" course, I was experimenting with different forms and fundamentals of pedagogy in an effort to cultivate the conditions that would encourage students to think differently about their digital lives and what it means to read Black history, culture, and community in the words and texts that surround them every day. "Digital Archives" was, ultimately, AADHum's only explicit teaching initiative and, therefore, an important vehicle through which we were able to explore what it means to foster and practice radically intentional pedagogy in Black DH.

What is Black DH Pedagogy?

Through its various initiatives, but especially in its undergraduate "Digital Archives" course, AADHum seized upon an opportunity to explore what happens when Black DH becomes a pedagogical imperative, not just a scholarly one. Black DH is a boundary-crossing, care-giving, intentional effort to pursue, critique, and/or engage digital use and making from the perspectives of Black life, history, and culture. Black DH pedagogy, therefore, is not simply the exposure of Black students to a slate of tools, skills, or methods. Instead, it begins and ends with centering Black people and invites us to consider Black DH as a mode of learning, teaching, making, and encountering the world such that Blackness, digitality, and humanity are always considered simultaneously and together. Integrating Black DH with undergraduate pedagogy means to cultivate and maintain an instructional space that is always both intentionally digital and intentionally Black.

Due to the ever-shifting nature of the FIRE program, in which courses are designed and hosted by individual faculty members and instructors, "Digital Archives" will never be offered again. In 2018, however, a small group of bright, energetic undergraduate students were willing to take a chance on the course, ask questions about Black folks and freedom, and try their hand at text encoding and data modeling. Their generosity and curiosity allowed us the privileged opportunity to experiment with and produce a model for Black DH pedagogy that can be translated to other DH programs and curricula. Black DH pedagogy teaches about the digital in ways that remain committed to: centering and affirming Black people as learners and teachers in the classroom; practicing care for students as whole persons; animating legacies of interdisciplinary power, resistance, and innovation in Black culture and community across the diaspora; and, moving beyond tools- or skills-focused instruction to engage theory-grounded critique of the impacts of emergent methods and technologies on the lives of Black people and their communities.

Affirming and Centering Black People as Learners and Teachers

Black DH pedagogy begins with a commitment to recognizing and supporting Black students as leaders in digital study and research. Situated in the FIRE program, "Digital Archives" was uniquely positioned to empower students as active agents not only in their own university education but in knowledge-making in the broader world. The design of a hands-on, research-oriented course afforded me an opportunity to affirm what I had come to see as a foundational tenet of Black DH: that Black people have historically been the most productive leaders at the ever-evolving edges of the digital frontier. With a small class comprised wholly of non-white students and a majority of Black students—a rarity at a predominantly white institution—it was both a pleasure and a privilege to design a course that centered my own students as learners and teachers not only in our shared classroom, but also throughout human history, cultural movement and change, and technological innovation.

The first step was inviting students into my research agenda in ways that made it their own. Rather than parceling out research tasks related to my own projects, I asked them to first consider if and how my research inquiry—*how do Black folks grapple with the question, "what does it mean to be free?"*—inspired curiosity in their own digital lives and worlds. I began the course by asking them to survey their digital surroundings and practices by paying close attention to the posts they liked, the images on their feeds, the op-eds they bookmarked and shared, and the memes that made them laugh. Each student started to identify trends in their digital engagement: Courtney Richardson and Ariana Lawson had spent a lot of time watching YouTube videos about natural hair care and styling; Sophia Crooks and Kayla Graham could not tire of reading audiences' responses to the latest Marvel film, *Black Panther*; and Alice Liu's interest in music meant that most of her encounters with Black communities online revolved around hip-hop's latest releases and most popular artists. Thus, the first weeks of the semester presumed that there was much to be learned from Black folks' discourse and engagement online, their unique study of which could, in turn, teach valuable lessons to others.

This move first reinforced the foundational premise that Black people have maintained a central role in propelling forward human history, cultural movement and change, and technological innovation. Rather than positioning them as passive receptacles for information in the classroom, it granted them agency in their learning and centered the students' own ideas and observations—rather than my own—in the instructional environment. Moreover, empowering students to direct their own research projects allowed them to position themselves at the center of Black innovation's forward thrust, as already-teachers in the present moment whenever they, too, engaged in digital practices online. They began to see themselves as participants in enduring legacies of Black knowledge-making.

For some, this reorientation toward students sounds daunting because it demands that pedagogues do their work differently. When students become researchers, the teacher's goal is transformed from lecturer to mentor, and the instructional focus shifts from content to method. With each successive week in the classroom, I spoke less and asked more. I prompted students to share what they had observed, which led us to discuss what questions they had next, and what they needed a particular tool to be able to do in order to address their queries. Their research guided the course more than any syllabus could and, over time, they grew to trust their own direction (Brown, 2017). I learned, too, how to adapt my other responsibilities accordingly. Rather than grading assignments for accuracy, I wrote rubrics that assessed: whether students were asking meaningful questions; if they were identifying and pursuing new directions prompted by their observations and findings; and, how clearly they could present their work to others.

Finding ways to position students as researchers and early scholars is foundational to Black DH pedagogy, because it lays claim to Black communities' prevailing influence on emergent and prevailing technologies. This pedagogical practice of upending the traditional teacher–student hierarchy reinforces how users continually innovate and challenge tools and technical affordances and, in doing so, help (re)make our digital worlds. At the same time, encouraging students to see themselves as powerful agents of intellectual production and research could plant seeds for the future of Black DH as a field.

Practicing Care for Students as Whole Persons

An approach to teaching about the digital in ways that position Black folks as our learners and teachers must necessarily be accompanied by other pedagogical considerations. In the shift for margin to center, Black folks demand and are afforded renewed care as whole and important persons. For Black students, especially, this praxis pays special attention to the ways in which they are not typically embraced as their whole selves, both inside and outside of the classroom. Countless studies abound regarding the reduction of Blackness and Black people to tired, racist tropes of violence, hypersexualization, laziness, and ignorance. Recent years, too, have seen multiple surges in media coverage of Black people in violent states of death and dying, usually at the hands of the state, reinforcing a narrative that suggests that Black life is only noteworthy when it is being ripped away (Dixon & Maddox, 2005). But in "Digital Archives," so many other aspects of Black life and living were affirmed as worthy of preservation, study, and analysis. Seemingly benign acts—like seeing a movie and sharing your reaction online, singing along to the latest hit by your favorite rapper, and the multi-day ritual of washing, styling, and protecting your hair—became the focus of students' work.

The insistence that the everyday-ness of Black life is worth caring about emerged as an important cornerstone of the Black DH learning environment, purposefully cultivated to affirm Black people's lives as valuable in all respects, not just for the purposes of intellectual study. Standard pedagogical practice often does not do much to alleviate the structural, systemic, and personal harms inflicted upon Black folks in the United States. By design, American public education is an imperial project that privileges select narratives and communities in order to maintain racism at home and abroad (Stratton, 2016), and self-reflective and self-reflexive education is often treated as a luxury rather than a human right for Black students. Practicing Black DH pedagogy requires educators to encounter their students as whole persons who are neither defined by nor beyond the reach of racism.

"Digital Archives" therefore taught me another valuable and challenging lesson: any recognition of Black students as fully human should also compel educators to exercise care for them—their learning, their health, and their overall wellbeing—in ways that extend beyond basic instruction. In the previous chapter, Catherine discussed at length the Black feminist traditions that grounded our team's ethics of care and feeding. The limits of our training as teachers can sometimes make these imperatives difficult to stomach, especially when many of us face our own challenges with financial stability, professional precarity, and mental health. But, there remain ways to practice care for Black students that fall within the scope of our teaching responsibilities.

In "Digital Archives," for example, this commitment meant, first, carefully promoting the course to clearly signal it was designed to center, see, believe, and affirm Black people, history, and culture. The course description was direct and unapologetic in its declarations:

> For Black and African Americans, whose voices have historically been silenced in traditional institutional archives, digital spaces can provide an opportunity for creative expression and argument that challenges dominant narratives. Situating itself at the intersections of African American history, rhetoric, and digital humanities, this research stream … considers how Black and African Americans create and engage in digital spaces that resist oppression, centralize blackness, and argue for freedom.

It was neither a coincidence nor a surprise when the class was small in number and overwhelmingly Black and brown. We had carved out a space where students did not have to mince words when talking frankly about racism, white supremacy, and power. To "curate your group … may seem counterintuitive to creating an inclusive space" (Souffrant, 2019), but this defiance of DH's presumed universal appeal is one strategy toward cultivating a safe and supportive learning environment for Black students and their allies.

Another strategy is to incorporate space for students' humanness into the structure and pacing of our teaching. I designed "Digital Archives" to model a rhythm and cadence of humanities research that prioritized time for exploration and play. Never before have I authored a syllabus with such flexibility and latitude in deadlines; I included an open revision policy that allowed students to revise and re-submit any assignment, for any reason, throughout the semester. Extended time was treated as an imperative, not an accommodation, to account for the unpredictable demands on students' time and energy and to further encourage them to play creatively with new tools and ideas, rather than merely mimicking how others may have historically used them. Intentionally creating and holding space for students to progress at a healthy pace also recognizes that, outside the classroom, Black people at play (even children, like Tamir Rice) are not safe; Black people are not allowed to be at their leisure without being presumed lazy; and play remains a necessary outlet for resistance, whether in the form of wordplay, dance, or other creative pursuits (Steele, 2016; Steele & Lu, 2018). From this perspective, extended time or flexible revision policies are not framed as accommodations but, instead, as a pedagogical structure for Black DH that reflects and respects Black history and culture.

As Saidiya Hartman reminds us, "Care is the antidote to violence" (*In the Wake: A Salon in Honor of Christina Sharpe*, 2017). By adopting pedagogical practices that care for students as whole humans, educators may move ever so slightly toward a world that poses less harm. We may also join in Black folks' ongoing struggle against racism, as "to teach… students from a spirit-permeated place of trust, love, and vulnerability is radical" (Lara, 2016, p. 185). Above all else, though, this commitment to affirming and centering students as both learners and teachers encourages them to recognize their power as knowledge-makers in an ever-shifting digital world, with much to contribute, build, and share.

Animating Legacies of Interdisciplinary Power, Resistance, and Innovation

Black DH pedagogy continues with a commitment to amplifying digital practices and spaces as complex, oft-contested sites of Black power, resistance, and innovation. Compared to other FIRE courses focused on equipping students with mastery of research techniques, "Digital Archives" considered technical skills of text encoding, data modeling, and discourse analysis to be a secondary priority. In the same way that AADHum grounded its workshops in critical approaches for graduate students and faculty, I sought to prepare undergraduates for skill-building by first exploring how technologies are developed and deployed within matrices of power. Before students opened the Atom text editor program or learned their first TEI element, they had already spent weeks diving deeply into the historical, cultural, and theoretical contexts that affirmed how and why those technologies might be relevant or provocative for anti-racist work. In other words, their introduction to DH framed new skills as cultural tools, not merely practical ones.

As a model for Black DH pedagogy, "Digital Archives" proposes that it is imperative for both educators and students to continually return to African American history and culture in order to build and sustain a Black DH class-room. With regards to digitality, in particular, legacies of power, resistance, and innovation emerge—and must remain—at the fore. Despite the prevalence of the "digital divide" narrative that often conflates systemic lack of access with lack of skill, Black people have always led the curve in technological innovation. A framework of Black technophilia allowed us to first explore the myriad ways in which Black people leverage, transform, and even transcend digital affordances to resist oppression, cultivate community, and play with the (re)distribution of power. "Digital Archives" therefore modeled a Black DH pedagogy that pre-empts any introduction to digital tools and methods with an honest and critical accounting of this history (Brock, 2020; Everett, 2002, 2009; Florini, 2016, 2019; Lu & Steele, 2019).

Firmly situating digital skill-building within the context of Black techno-philia dispels the racist notion that the skills students can learn are a panacea, generously bestowed upon them by (often) non-Black instructors (me included). This can powerfully shift Black students' perspectives on their own education, affirming that developing technical and technological skills is more than a new strategic approach to professional success in increasingly hostile economies; it is a tradition passed down by their communities. The framework also encourages students to critique DH tools and engage them with curiosity and playfulness, seeing the potential for invention and innovation and honoring the legacies of so many other Black users that have come before.

By the time I began introducing students to the tags, elements, and work-flows that shape the Text Encoding Initiative (TEI), they were ready to appraise it carefully and honestly, and with a clear sense of ethical—as well as techni-cal—purpose (Heil, 2016; Bailey, 2015). They found that some of the TEI "best practices" did not align with their goals, so they instituted encoding habits to honor Black history and, in doing so, created better, richer, more provocative digital models of Black discourse.

For example, Richardson and Lawson's interest in Black users' discussions of natural hair and hair styling compelled them to encode a tweet posted by actress and singer Zendaya Maree Stoermer Coleman, after entertainment show host Giuliana Rancic criticized the way she had styled her hair for the Oscars award ceremony in February 2015. TEI markup requires only basic metadata for a digi-tal surrogate; an encoder can offer only a title, minimal publication information, and some description of the original source and still produce a digital file that is considered valid and complete. So, as shown in Figure 4.1, a "complete" TEI header for the digital edition began like this:

```
<teiHeader>
      <fileDesc>
            <titleStmt>
                        <title>Tweet by Zendaya</title>
            </titleStmt>
            <publicationStmt>
                        <p>Published by University of Maryland, College Park</p>
            </publicationStmt>
            <sourceDesc>
                        <p>Original Twitter post by Zendaya on February 14, 2015</p>
            </sourceDesc>
      </fileDesc>
</teiHeader>
```

FIGURE 4.1 A student's default TEI header for a valid digital edition.

This first attempt at encoding a TEI header for the digital edition taught them the basics of TEI tags, nesting structure, and the importance of metadata. But they quickly realized they needed to exceed the bare minimum in order to achieve their goals: producing a critical digital surrogate of Zendaya's tweet, as well as honoring the spirit of Black resistance she enacted in posting it. In the <titleStmt> alone, they recognized two key opportunities. First, they could be intentional about the way they titled the digital edition. They knew that news headlines and media narratives of events in Black communities shape public perception. So, they decided to use <title> in ways that explicitly affirmed Zendaya's response to Rancic's criticism. Second, they could supply extensive authorship information within <titleStmt> to credit those whose labor contributed to the digital edition (James, 2017). Both history and contemporary politics remind us that the American people have consistently failed to recognize and compensate Black people for their labor—from chattel slavery to the contemporary prison industrial complex (Alexander, 2012). With this knowledge, Richardson and Lawson realized that it was necessary to utilize non-required TEI elements and tags (such as assigning xml identifiers (xml:id) and encoding <respStmt>[4]) to account for the many layers of labor involved in digital work, from the overwhelmingly Black and brown staff who maintain and prepare the facilities in which they worked, to their own peers who helped us collect, transcribe, and encode the material.

Accordingly, the TEI header for the digital edition evolved. The digital edition's fuller <titleStmt>, as depicted in Figure 4.2, exceeded what is required by TEI but it became the absolute bare minimum for their projects. They agreed that the tool needed to adapt to the kind of work they wanted to do and the claims they wanted their scholarly editions to make. Working as researchers and encoders, the students affirmed that they could be active agents rather than passive receptors in their DH education, and that they were empowered to make encoding decisions based on the principles and practices central to their own communities.

```
<titleStmt>
        <title type="main">Zendaya's powerful response to ignorant commentary about her Oscars hairstyle</title>
        <title type="sub">Digital Edition</title>
        <author>
                <persName xml:id="CSR">Courtney Richardson</persName>
                <persName xml:id="AL">Ariana Lawson</persName>
                <orgName xml:id="ADH">African American History, Culture, and Digital Humanities
                        (<abbr>AADHum</abbr>) Initiative</orgName>
        </author>
        <respStmt>
                <resp>Encoded by</resp>
                        <persName ref="#AL">Ariana Lawson</persName>
                        <persName ref="#CSR">Courtney Richardson</persName>
        </respStmt>
        <respStmt>
                <resp>TEI instruction provided by</resp>
                        <persName xml:id="JLU">Jessica H. Lu</persName>
        </respStmt>
        <respStmt>
                <resp>Original TEI template provided by</resp>
                        <persName xml:id="RV">Raffaele Viglianti</persName>
        </respStmt>
        <respStmt>
                <resp>Instructional spaces maintained by</resp>
                        <orgName>Facilities staff, University of Maryland, College Park</orgName>
        </respStmt>
</titleStmt>
```

FIGURE 4.2 A student's expanded TEI Header for a Black DH digital edition.

The foundations laid in "Digital Archives" supported students to understand and appreciate Black people as technological dissenters, innovators, and teachers, leaving behind footsteps that they, too, could follow. They further perceived themselves to wield great responsibility in exercising their new skillsets and sought, at every turn, to push tools forward in ways that were sensitive to the legacies and needs of Black communities. I took great pride in not only watching and guiding them to learn how to encode texts but also in seeing them develop and practice self-agency in leveraging new tools to make cultural interventions in real-time. In other courses, too, I believe it is possible for Black DH pedagogy to resist the marginalization of Black students by beginning with Black people's sustained legacies of digital engagement and innovation. Doing so emboldens Black students and their peers to see Black folks as makers and creators not just of digital content, but of the very tools that they are using.

Grounding Tools and Skills Instruction in Theory-Informed Critique

The third commitment of Black DH pedagogy further decentralizes tools- and skills-focused instruction by giving equal—if not primary—weight to theory that contextualizes and critiques technologies' impacts on Black people and their communities. Whether in DH writ large, or in the FIRE program, technical expertise is often championed as an enviable gateway toward valuable rewards or acclaim. But, I was firm in my determination to make sure that "Digital

Archives" was not a "TEI class." In "Digital Archives," AADHum sought to reframe digital skills as vehicles toward greater aims that can potentially far surpass students' academic and professional goals. Students may have enrolled in the course thinking that, by learning how to encode texts, they could position themselves as job candidates with programming skills and experience. But they left the course with an understanding of text encoding as a critical method for reading, analyzing, and modeling Black language that invokes lessons pertaining to how our world collects, interprets, and tells stories about Black people and their experiences.

In order to contextualize digital tools and methods in this way, I took great care in introducing students to theory and scholarly literature about Black life—digital and otherwise. They learned about TEI not by reading the *Journal of the Text Encoding Initiative*, but by reading about the role of archives in dehumanizing Black women (Fuentes, 2016; Hartman, 2008); the importance of community archiving (Jules, 2018); the power of archives to speculate new futures (Caswell, 2014); and the politics of citation (Ahmed, 2013).[5] This humanities research prepared them to identify the myriad ways in which text encoding can be complicit in diminishing and dehumanizing Black life and scholarship, as well as building digital archives that replicate racist violence.[6]

What I did not anticipate, however, was how grounding skills instruction in Black theory would compel students to use their new tools to point others in the same directions. Much to my delight, scholarly text encoding became a mechanism by which the "Digital Archives" students started to read differently online; they mimicked and latched on to the practice of providing more and more context—intellectual, historical, and cultural—to what they were doing. The quality of their attention shifted, along with their motivation; reading became less about themselves, personally, and more about their communities. No longer were they asking, "Did I understand what I just read?" Instead, they wondered, "What information can or should I give a reader to help them understand this as I do?" Rather than asking them to simply absorb or consume the content of the course, I asked them to share it—and, in doing so, participate in the exchange of knowledge-making and theory-building.

Grounded in the principles of Black DH pedagogy, encoding allowed them to do that. When Liu read the lyrics of "Be Free," a 2014 song by artist J. Cole, she wanted present and future fans—especially non-Black ones—to understand how certain verses actively demanded justice for 18-year-old Michael Brown, who was shot and killed by a police officer on August 9, 2014, in Ferguson, Missouri. Part of the song samples verbal testimony from Brown's friend, Dorian Johnson. When encoding the lyrics, Liu decided to use the <supplied> tag to ensure that both Brown's and Johnson's names, and the injustices committed against them, could not be overlooked.

As we <supplied reason="say-names">Dorian Johnson and Michael Brown</supplied> took off running I ducked and hid for my life, because I was fearing for my life. I hid behind the first car I saw. My friend <supplied reason="say-names">Michael Brown</supplied>, he kept running, and he told me to keep running because he feared for me too.

FIGURE 4.3 Creative misuse of TEI <supplied> for Black DH.

While Liu's encoding choices depicted in Figure 4.3 appear simple, they were experimental, unconventional, and significant. The verbal testimony sampled in the song did not explicitly include the speaker's name, nor Michael Brown's. She felt that a listener needed to know and understand the context—Michael Brown's murder—as well as the people involved to fully grasp the meaning of the passage, or appreciate the importance of modeling the lyrics in digital form as part of a corpus about Black freedom. Liu also decided that straightforward use of TEI would be insufficient; she decided to adapt the "supplied" tag for her own purposes. While traditionally used to insert text in the event of illegible or damaged writing in the original source, she opted to deploy <supplied> to underscore that these young Black men's names deserved to be said, their lives affirmed, and the injustices against them recognized by any future reader or listener.[7] As an interpreter and modeler, introduced to DH methods that could not be divorced from Black theory or history, she decided to *supply* what she felt to be crucial information—even if that isn't how *supply* was designed or intended to be used. When so many Black men and women are murdered, often without consequences for the perpetrators, it becomes easy for most audiences to forget their names—or, worse yet, ignore them. Liu aimed to use TEI to build digital collections that diligently recorded their names and kept their lives at the forefront.[8]

Encoding practices and playfulness such as this allowed students to distill important lessons they had learned from Black thinkers, embed them in a digital edition, and share them with others who do not have the privilege or access to the same kind of education they do.

By consistently leading with—and returning to—African Americanist research, Black DH pedagogy enriches DH with new theories, concepts, and frameworks. It ensures that DH instruction is not a technical effort toward mastery nor a mere rung on a ladder toward some job or career but rather a holistic education that encourages students to reckon with how, why, and by whom tools can be used to support their communities. It further affirms that Black life, history, and culture can be at the center of intellectual progress, as the field of DH evolves to grapple with new methods of research and modes of teaching. By centering Blackness in Black DH pedagogy, we can show our students that there is a place for them not only in DH's present, but in its future.

KEY LESSONS: RADICALLY INTENTIONAL BLACK DH PEDAGOGY

Black DH pedagogy is a humanities-informed orientation toward teaching about the digital that remains committed to: centering and affirming Black people as learners and teachers in the classroom; practicing care for students as whole persons; animating legacies of interdisciplinary power, resistance, and innovation in Black culture and community across the diaspora; and, moving beyond tools- or skills-focused instruction to engage theory-grounded critique of the impacts of emergent methods and technologies on the lives of Black people and their communities.

Black DH pedagogy does not divorce tools and skills from the Black life, history, and culture that produces, innovates, and challenges them.

Black DH pedagogy aims to equip Black learners, especially, with the practical and conceptual knowledge to understand the inextricable role of technology in Black life.

Black DH pedagogy practices care for its learners, prioritizing the long-term wellbeing of Black digital users and makers as essential to the longevity and sustainability of Black life and culture.

Black DH pedagogy does not naturally occur in the presence of Black people or digital learning; it requires an intentional effort to cultivate a holistic pedagogical practice that centers and affirms Black people, Black digitality, and Black life.

Teaching Black DH with Radical Intentionality

For one year, AADHum had the rare opportunity to collaboratively build an undergraduate learning environment that was intentionally digital and intentionally Black. In "Digital Archives," we created a Black DH classroom that centered—not merely included—Black students. DH skills may be prized assets on the job market, but their value soars well beyond professional advancement when accompanied by intentional Black DH pedagogy that seeks "historical [and] sociological depth" as well as "computational depth." Black DH pedagogy is therefore an effort to move students toward what Ruha Benjamin calls "deep learning … a historically and sociologically grounded approach [that] can open up possibilities. It can create new settings. It can encode new values and build on critical intellectual traditions that have continually developed insights and strategies grounded in justice" (Johnson, 2020).

In "Digital Archives," I taught students how to encode scholarly editions, but I also endeavored to show them: how DH tools could help read, work, and learn for their communities; how it feels to be seen and cared for as Black women and women of color in academic spaces; how to honor the histories that shape their lives and futures; and how to produce research that affirms their experiences. The course, therefore, emerged as one of the strongest models AADHum built in its efforts to lay foundations for a Black DH community. Through "Digital Archives," we not only introduced a new digital skillset to undergraduate students, but also created and held space to critique and confront how white supremacy, racism, and power impact everyday life, and particularly the lives and living of Black people.

Sadly, "Digital Archives" will never happen again. The FIRE program is structured in such a way that its research streams are closely tied to the program's faculty; when a faculty member departs, the stream ends (if it is not inherited by another faculty member with the same research goals or methods). When my time with AADHum ended in early 2019, "Digital Archives" was removed from FIRE's catalog.

But I carry the principles of Black DH pedagogy with me. The lessons I learned in my time with AADHum have translated to new environments, even without the institutional support to focus exclusively on Black DH research and teaching. After leaving AADHum, I was lucky to move into a new role at the University of Maryland as Associate Director of Design Cultures & Creativity (DCC), a living-learning program in the Honors College. In my fourth year with DCC, I assumed the position of Interim Director and have overseen the evolution of the program into one that grounds students' experimentation with emergent technologies in rich counter-dominant histories and cultures; affirms the necessity of intentional creative practices in increasingly violent and precarious worlds; and, encourages students to pursue opportunities in which they can be empowered to imagine, design, and build just futures. DCC is an interdisciplinary program and has therefore extended my AADHum work in exciting ways. Whether the students are committed to communication, information science, computer science, engineering, studio art, architecture, history, American Studies, gender studies, sustainability … the same fundamental principles apply. Radical intentionality means centering Black people and culture wherever human life is the subject of inquiry and investigation; recognizing and affirming the knowledge created and shared by Black scholars and thinkers whenever research methods and practices are taught; and, contextualizing the evolution of digital technology within broader legacies of Black technophilia and cyberculture. Radical intentionality means that Black DH pedagogy can be brought forth into unexpected spaces and places in the undergraduate experience by Black teachers and their allies.

FUNDAMENTAL PRINCIPLES OF BLACK DH PEDAGOGY

Trust learners as creators, "hackers," and innovators of digital tools, even if that means we teach tools in unconventional ways. Too often, teachers assume a role of intellectual and creative authority in the classroom that discounts students' knowledge and potential. Black DH pedagogy strives to recognize and affirm learners' power, especially as digital users and creators, by shifting our pedagogical orientation from instruction to mentorship. By further approaching digital skills and tools as opportunities for change and disruption, we can honor histories of Black technophilia, extend legacies of Black technological innovation, and enliven DH as a field responsive to human creativity.

Create and maintain space for rest as integral to learning. Black DH pedagogy seeks to care for Black life by actively providing for rest. In defiance of capitalist expectations for constant productivity, especially from non-white and poor people, we carve out and enforce moments of intentional pause—whether by instituting breaks throughout class meetings, proposing no-contact/communication hours, observing Black cultural rituals or holidays, or scheduling regular/semi-regular rest days without class meetings or assignments.

Encourage experimentation and revision over accuracy and mastery. Black DH pedagogy believes joy and play to be inherently good, especially for Black people and Black children who are presumed adult—in sexuality, in accountability, in responsibility—well before they reach adulthood. We see the opportunity to make mistakes, be wrong, correct, and adapt as a privilege so often denied to Black people, but easily extended in Black DH pedagogy through assessment practices that prioritize experimentation and revision over accuracy and mastery. Black DH pedagogy thrives on scaffolded assignments, collaborative work, and skills-based training modules/tutorials that invite students to try new tools and methods without assessing their mastery of them.

Create opportunities for community. Building on strong foundations of collaboration in DH work, Black DH pedagogy can further move away from individualized teaching and learning toward more community-centered practices. By crafting exercises and assignments that encourage learners to work together, forge connections, share resources, and exchange specialized knowledge, we can affirm Black and indigenous cultural practices of kinship and mutual aid. An intentional approach to the classroom as a community undertaking, rather than a competitive space for individualized learning, also serves to build networks of survival—both intellectual and social—for Black learners and practitioners.

Contextualize digital tools and skills in Black knowledge and scholarship, both digital and non-digital alike. Understanding that Black life and digitality are always intertwined demands that DH learning is enriched by humanities teachings in related fields, including Black Studies, African American Studies, history, communication, information science, English, queer studies, and Women's, gender, and sexuality studies. To better grasp the integral role of technology, Black DH pedagogy requires an interdisciplinary effort to learn about Black life, history, and culture.

Remove as many barriers to learning as possible. Black DH pedagogy asks us to identify obstacles in learners' efforts to attain knowledge and, whenever possible, remove them. Rather than requiring licensed software, opt to teach new skills using free, open-source programs. Rather than requiring that learners rent or purchase textbooks or training materials, search for costless alternatives. Seek to present information dynamically in a variety of different formats—audiovisual, textual, hands-on. Create contact opportunities beyond the formal classroom environment, whether via in-person or virtual appointments or "student hours." In recognition of the resource-hoarding that systematically undercuts Black people's efforts to attain education, we can actively seek to make Black DH learning as accessible as possible.

RADICAL REFLECTIONS FOR INTENTIONAL BLACK DH TEACHERS

- What knowledge or insights do these learners bring to bear upon this tool/technology?
- How can this tool/skill help learners understand elements, experiences, or phenomena of Black life differently?
- How does Black life, history, and/or culture inform the use, affordances, and/or impact of this skill/tool?
- How can this tool/skill be weaponized against Black life or Black people? What safeguards or innovations must be pursued to protect against its (mis)use?
- Which Black thinkers, designers, artists, and makers can help learners understand this tool/skill/idea differently?
- What conversation exists only in this room/space, and how can I help foster it?

- How does my course—in content, structure, assessment, and practice—enact intentional care for learners' lives and overall wellbeing?
- Why am I a valuable voice in this learning experience? What are my contributions—and my limits—in this community?
- Whose voice and/or expertise is needed here? Whom can invite to share knowledge and resources?

Notes

1 When AADHum and FIRE forged their partnership, "Digital Archives" was the first humanities research course in the program. At the time of this writing, FIRE continues to focus primarily on natural science, social science, and applied technology research.

2 See Appendix B for an excerpted syllabus.

3 TEI is a widely used markup language, especially among textual and literary scholars. It comprises thousands of elements, attributes, and tags for encoding text-based artifacts, with a focus on the ordered hierarchy of content objects (OHCO). TEI also refers to the consortium of its users, a global community of encoders who employ the language and challenge it to grow with users' evolving research needs. See https://tei-c.org.

4 According to the Text Encoding Initiative P5 Guidelines, <respStmt> "supplies a statement of responsibility for the intellectual content of a text, edition, recording, or series, where the specialized elements for authors, editors, etc. do not suffice or do not apply. May also be used to encode information about individuals or organizations which have played a role in the production or distribution of a bibliographic work." See www.tei-c.org/release/doc/tei-p5-doc/en/html/ref-respStmt.html.

5 The politics of citation are also continually affirmed by countless scholars on Twitter, with Black users especially employing the hashtags #CiteASista (Dr. Brittany Williams and Dr. Joan Collier), #CiteHerWork and #TheGrayTest (Dr. Kishonna Gray), and #CiteBlackWomen (Dr. Christen A. Smith) to credit and amplify scholarship by Black women.

6 Our work has since spurred a new project, a joint venture between myself and Caitlin Pollock, a digital librarian at the University of Michigan, to design a TEI schema that upholds Black feminist practices.

7 It's important to note that those faithful to TEI would likely be dissatisfied with this example, as it does not conform with TEI best practices. Despite trumpeting the language as flexible, the community altogether maintains a general commitment to using TEI in the ways it was "meant" to be used. Relevant to this particular example, the TEI Guidelines have since been amended and expanded to include a new element, <standOff>, which was not previously available during the time of "Digital Archives." The TEI Council and community have now designated <standOff> as the proper channel for encoding contextual information in TEI projects. At the time of this writing, the TEI Council and a small sub-committee are also in the process of developing long-overdue markup language for computer mediated communication.

8 We were continually reminded to sustain this effort by "Hell You Talmbout," a 2015 song by artists Janelle Monae and Wondaland Records. The song alternates between reciting the names of murdered Black men and women and reminding listeners to "say his name"/"say her name." See www.youtube.com/watch?v=fumaCsQ9wKw.

References

Ahmed, S. (2013, September 11). *Making Feminist Points.* https://feministkilljoys.com/2013/09/11/making-feminist-points/

Alexander, M. (2012). *The new Jim Crow: Mass incarceration in the age of colorblindness.* New Press.

Bailey, M. Z. (2015). #transform(ing)DH writing and research: An autoethnography of digital humanities and feminist ethics. *Digital Humanities Quarterly, 9*(2).

Brock, A. (2020). *Distributed blackness.* NYU Press.

Brown, A. M. (2017). *Emergent strategy: Shaping change, changing worlds.* AK Press.

Browne, S. (2015). *Dark matters: On the surveillance of Blackness.* Duke University Press.

Caswell, M. (2014). Inventing new archival imaginaries: Theoretical foundations for identity-based community archives. In D. Daniel & A. Levi (Eds.), *Identity palimpsests: Archiving ethnicity in the U.S. and Canada* (pp. 35–55). Litwin Books.

Caswell, M. (2017). Teaching to dismantle white supremacy in archives. *The Library Quarterly, 87*(3), 222–235. https://doi.org/10.1086/692299

Dixon, T. L., & Maddox, K. B. (2005). Skin tone, crime news, and social reality judgments: Priming the stereotype of the dark and dangerous Black criminal. *Journal of Applied Social Psychology, 35*(8), 1555–1570. https://doi.org/10.1111/j.1559-1816.2005.tb02184.x

Drake, J. M. (2016, October 22). Liberatory archives: Towards belonging and believing. *Medium.* https://medium.com/on-archivy/liberatory-archives-towards-belonging-and-believing-part-1-d26aaeb0edd1

Everett, A. (2002). The revolution will be digitized: Afrocentricity and the digital public sphere. *Social Text, 20*(2), 125–146. https://doi.org/10.1215/01642472-20-2_71-125

Everett, A. (2009). *Digital diaspora: A race for cyberspace.* SUNY Press.

Florini, S. (2016). Tweets, tweeps, and signifyin': Communication and cultural performance on "Black Twitter". *Television & New Media, 15*(3), 223–237. https://doi.org/10.1177/1527476413480247

Florini, S. (2019). *Beyond HASHTAGS: Racial politics and Black digital networks.* New York University Press.

Fuentes, M. J. (2016). *Dispossessed lives: Enslaved women, violence, and the archive.* University of Pennsylvania Press.

Gallon, K. (2016). Making a case for the Black digital humanities. In *Debates in the digital humanities.* http://dhdebates.gc.cuny.edu/debates/text/55

Hartman, S. (2008). Venus in two acts. *Small Axe, 12*(2), 1–14.

Heil, J. (2016, February 1). Why we TEI. Digital Scholarship: Projects & Pedagogy. http://digitalscholarship.ohio5.org/2016/02/why-we-tei-2/

In the Wake: A Salon in Honor of Christina Sharpe. (2017). https://vimeo.com/203012536

James, R. (2017). A non-zero sum game. It's Her Factory. www.its-her-factory.com/2017/12/a-non-zero-sum-game-some-thoughts-on-the-politics-of-scholarship/

Johnson, K. (2020). Ruha Benjamin on deep learning. *VentureBeat.* https://venturebeat.com/2020/04/29/ruha-benjamin-on-deep-learning-computational-depth-without-sociological-depth-is-superficial-learning/.

Jules, B. (2018, January 5). We're All Bona Fide. https://medium.com/on-archivy/were-all-bona-fide-f502bdaea029

Lara, I. (2016). From the four directions: The dreaming, birthing, healthing mother on fire. In A. P. Gumbs, C. Martens, & M. Williams (Eds.), *Revolutionary mothering: Love on the front lines* (pp. 185–189). PM Press.

Lu, J. H., & Steele, C. K. (2019). 'Joy is resistance': Cross-platform resilience and (re) invention of Black oral culture online. *Information, Communication & Society, 22*(6), 823–837.

Noble, S. U. (2018). *Algorithms of oppression: How search engines reinforce racism.* New York University Press.

Souffrant, K. (2019, November 14). Putting ego aside: Strategies for building inclusive Black academic spaces. African American Intellectual History Society. www.aaihs. org/putting-ego-aside-strategies-for-building-inclusive-black-academic-spaces/

Steele, C., & Lu, J. (2018). Defying death: Black joy as resistance online. In Z. Papacharissi (Ed.), *A networked self and birth, life, death* (pp. 143–159). https://doi. org/10.4324/9781315202129-9

Steele, C. K. (2016). The digital barbershop: Blogs and online oral culture within the African American community. *Social Media + Society, 2*(4), 1–10.

Stratton, C. (2016). *Education for empire: American schools, race, and the paths of good citizenship.* University of California Press.

5

WHEN AND HOW TO WALK AWAY

Catherine Knight Steele, Jessica H. Lu, and Kevin C. Winstead

As a team, we worked to build something for our community, pouring all of ourselves into it for more than three years. There was intense pride in the community that we created and the intentional work that we did to make it a sustainable project at the University of Maryland that would have extensions across the country. We saw how more and more Black digital humanities (DH) projects and centers were being funded. We were keenly aware of how our conference, workshops, and reading groups intimately touched the lives of countless researchers, students, and community members. And then, we all felt how swiftly we could be dismissed from this work. Our expendability as individual laborers within a larger system was made clear to us. In this chapter, we discuss the harsh reality of doing the good work within a bureaucratic system that often seems designed for that good work not to exist. We each trace the story of our hirings and departures from the African American History, Culture, and Digital Humanities Initiative (AADHum) to think more carefully about the precarity of labor within Black DH and how we, as scholars, faculty, students, and grant administrators, can do better by the folks doing this work. We recognize that we are taking a risk in writing these personal, and often painful, narratives. We also recognize that the truths we write below were experienced differently by others. We write this not to negate their truth but simply to give voice to our own and draw valuable lessons from what others might see as traumatic experiences. Care for both ourselves and others embarking on their own Black DH journeys requires working through the feelings we carried about the end of our time with AADHum. Here, we reflect with pride on our work and hold space for accountability about how we departed.

DOI: 10.4324/9781003299134-6

Catherine: "Too Junior to Get the Credit"

In the spring of 2016, I traveled to the Rutgers University campus to attend the *Digital Blackness* conference. I was enthusiastic about meeting and networking with other scholars who studied social media and practitioners who were often the subjects of our inquiry. It was there that I first met one of my personal heroes, Patricia Hill Collins, when she attended my panel, and I presented research that would later evolve into my book, *Digital Black Feminism*. But I also saw that conference as an opportunity to strategically introduce myself to faculty from the University of Maryland, a school that held a top Communication program and, separately, was engaging in building strength in digital studies. I attended a presentation by Sheri Parks and Neil Fraistat about their new grant, *Synergies Among African American History and Culture and Digital Humanities*. We chatted after their talk about the project and what they hoped to accomplish. When I heard from Dr. Parks a few weeks later and accepted an invitation to attend the grant's launch in Maryland, I had no idea I was flying out for an interview. But, at the launch, Dr. Parks made clear I was under consideration to direct what we would later call AADHum.

The grant Principal Investigator (PI) and Co-PIs had a formal search process for a director in the fall of 2015, wherein they sought a senior scholar to lead the initiative. That search did not yield favorable results. As I would later understand, it is challenging to persuade a tenured senior scholar that they should run a major grant program while not receiving credit as a PI. Though it requires tremendous teaching and research, this work is seen primarily as service—and service work, while fulfilling in many ways, does not lead to promotion. However, as a very junior scholar sitting at dinner with college deans and the heads of major campus centers and institutes, the idea of running a multi-million dollar grant was enticing, primarily because it would be at the University of Maryland—a school where I applied for tenure track positions twice and never made it to the first round of phone interviews. They asked if I was interested in pursuing a formal application. That night, I called my partner, most trusted colleagues, and friends to raise my concerns. My primary concern was not about the amount of labor that would be required, the ways that such a position would pull me away from my research, nor how my time with the grant would undermine my ability to build a relationship with my colleagues in a new department. At this stage of my career, I did not know these were problems that should concern me. I believed then, as I did for the next several years, that the senior folks around me—especially the Black women—would protect me. My concern was, simply, would they see my work fitting closely enough with DH to hire me? I did not make or build anything; I did my social media analysis and coding by hand rather than using computational tools. As Kevin discussed in the second chapter of this book, my hire pointed toward a redefinition of what got to count as Black DH work. It also signaled recognition by the Black folks at the helm of the grant that having someone who was deeply committed to Black studies, Black theories, and Black people lead the project might be more important than having someone who could teach DH tools.

However, returning to what should have been my concerns, the story of my hire at AADHum signals a challenge for DH and Black DH projects. The skills, expertise, and enthusiasm needed to imagine and build Black DH often exists most strongly among junior scholars. Those at the start of their careers tend to be less invested in discipline, often have had more training in computational and design thinking, and are not yet bound to the bureaucracies of institutions that can be a hindrance to creating DH projects centered on Blackness. Yet, these junior scholars are also in the university's most precarious position as faculty. Their work is done in preparation for tenure review. They often work outside their departments, yet are expected to meet the department and discipline-specific requirements for tenure and promotion. They also hold relatively little institutional power and cannot push back against the demands of other stakeholders whose commitments to care and intentionality may differ. Their ability to advocate for themselves or their graduate assistants is impacted by their need to attain a favorable review and keep within the good graces of more senior faculty and administrators. So, we need bright junior scholars to lead innovative initiatives in Black DH. Yet, those same scholars routinely do not receive the support and protection required to advance their careers and keep them well.

As director of AADHum, I hired my team—many of whom were not the type of candidates originally imagined for their positions. Some of the graduate students that worked on our grant had never touched digital tools before. Yet, by the end of my time with the project, they taught those tools paired with a deep understanding and passion for Black history and culture. We strayed away from the original plan of working with many campus centers and institutes that were outlined in the grant proposal, recognizing that ultimately our priority was to partner with both people and organizations whose values aligned with our own, even if they did not have a long CV or name recognition among academic big-hitters.

After three years of delivering on grant objectives, building a stellar team and national reputation for the college, and successfully chairing the first Black DH conference, it was time to figure out how AADHum would live on past the initial grant funding. I remained in close contact with the new grant Co-PIs (Drs. Parks and Friastat had since moved on) who wished to write a new grant proposal to extend AADHum for another three years. Together, we drafted objectives, and I provided evidence of our success to include in the final report. In addition, I met with college business managers, as I always had, to ensure the financial health of the grant was intact. However, when I asked whether, after three years of demonstrating my value to the project, I should be promoted to Co-PI for the subsequent round of funding—whether I could receive the kind of credit I needed for my own prospects toward tenure and promotion—I was told I was "too junior" for such a role.

I was not too junior to do the work; I was, it seemed too junior to receive the credit.

For many senior administrators at universities, cultural heritage sites, and in the eyes of many funders, junior faculty are necessary laborers in their pursuit of Black DH work. Yet these same individuals, along with the graduate students and post-doctoral associates often hired in place of more expensive tenure-track faculty lines, are ultimately expendable. Part of AADHum's unique origin story is that the college administration led the request for outside funding, tying the grant's success to the college's success. Yet, this same factor that proved valuable in securing outside funding also leads us to an essential question about the future of externally funded and institutionally supported Black DH work. When Black members of the team ask for what they need and have earned—when they extend care to themselves—how will those in power meet those requests? How will the Black DH projects predicated on a praxis of Black feminist care and Black liberation deal with the real material needs of the Black folks whose labor secures funding in the first place?

When I left AADHum in 2019, it was one of the saddest days of my professional life. I spent the previous nine months advocating for my team of graduate students and post-docs to have their contracts extended. I watched each one walk away from the project for a host of different reasons. Some left to accept fantastic new opportunities, some were never provided a rationale for why they were not being kept on board, and for others, their final weeks on the grant were filled with a deep sense of betrayal that still haunts me to this day. This project occupied far more time and energy than I should have allowed, given my responsibilities to my family and tenure case. In the spring of 2019, when I took my negotiated research leave to work on my book, I never imagined I would not return to my position in the fall. Those few months in between provided me with critical lessons I hope to pass on to those planning to take on their own Black DH work.

Black DH Grants should not be written simply to supplement salaries that require more hard-budget from the university for continued success. There is always a shortage of funding. There are always more faculty lines needed in a given department, more courses that need to be taught, and more students that need advisors. And, there are always multiple factions within institutions vying for the small bucket of resources. Leaders, though, cannot ignore this challenge and responsibility in managing the shortage purely through temporary outside funding. Putting the onus back on faculty to self-fund will privilege certain disciplines and create situations of precarity for faculty hired in those situations. Kicking the can down the road has consequences for the can and for the next person who must pick it up.

Titles and status cannot be the primary driving force in who is given external funding for Black DH projects. Funding agencies may rightly consider whether those applying for grants will be able to get the support they need outside of their grant funding to continue their proposed work. Likewise, indicators of support from college administrators may provide a softer landing for new grant holders in getting their projects off the ground. However, if funding is reserved for the institutions and senior faculty whose funding already outpaces junior folks, HBCUs, regional colleges, etc., how does that ultimately extend equity in the field?

Junior scholars may be better equipped to run your projects, but they must be given credit for this work and protected via institutional support. I don't suggest that the appropriate solution to precarity is to exclude students and junior faculty from Black DH. On the contrary, those who are taking the lead on these projects and those at funding agencies who see the value in this work must work to build a praxis of care into how we hire, retain and support junior staff. This will not happen by junior folks advocating for it. Instead, our promotion guidelines, the terms of our postdoctoral contracts, and the kind of professional development offered to graduate assistants and professional track faculty must be written and protected by those in a position to take such risks.

When a project's values of care and Black liberation are no longer seen through the actions of those in charge, it may be time to walk away. Walking away from funding in the humanities seems absurd. In a time where more humanities scholars are recognizing that the path forward is based on our ability to secure external grants, much like our colleagues in STEM and social science, it seems laughable that the right decision is to terminate a successful project or to walk away just as more funding comes in. Yet, I learned that how you walk away must be as intentional as how you manage the project.

Jessica: "Except Me"

I needed a push. It had been almost a full calendar year since I had defended my prospectus—a document I had hastily assembled over the course of two weeks, writing in 22-hour spurts with little sleep and barely any sustenance—and I had made little to no progress on my dissertation. I was in the fifth year of my Ph.D. journey and I was exhausted, unmotivated, and disenchanted. Above all else, I was uninspired. My advisor may have sensed it and was worried for me; or, she was exercising the mentorship muscles she was most well-known for: searching out leads for her advisees and creating opportunities for them to succeed in ways the academy recognizes most clearly as success. In late fall 2016, she let me know that a new grant had come to the University of Maryland and the College of Arts and Humanities, and she thought I would be the perfect fit for one of their two Graduate Assistant positions. It was about "African American digital humanities," she said, which was perfect since I was studying Black rhetorics of freedom and was "tech-savvy."

I did not know, at the time, how intellectually unprepared I was for my graduate assistantship with AADHum and my impending entrée into DH. I was just excited about the potential of connecting my expertise in antebellum and emancipation era Black language practices to more contemporary analyses, and carrying forward methods of rhetorical criticism into digital spaces. Most importantly, however, I was eager to experience a new kind of graduate assistantship; I was tired of being paid so little to teach so many students each semester, and the role with AADHum meant I could take home a bigger paycheck without sacrificing my energy to more teaching overloads. I interviewed for the position as soon as I was able and was thrilled to get it. I sensed that I was out of my depth, intellectually, after just one conversation with Catherine and Jovonne, but I was confident that I would work hard, pick things up quickly, and could serve AADHum by simply getting things done—the kind of immediate-gratification work that Ph.D. students so rarely get to enjoy. My excitement was spoiled only just a little when I allowed myself to recognize—with the help of my friends and fellow peers, who bristled ever so slightly at the news—that I had gotten this novel opportunity because my advisor had decided it was already mine. With her connections, insider knowledge, and favor, I had been given the chance at an assistantship that no one else even knew was available.

Once I was brought on board, it became abundantly clear what a privileged position I had seized. Surely, I was not the only "tech-savvy" (read: "born after 1985") graduate student on campus with research interests related to Black history and culture, but I had been chosen to be a part of this burgeoning effort to establish and foster a Black DH community at University of Maryland, and beyond. The work was invigorating and inspiring, and it pushed me forward not only in my professional development (as I began to add administrative credentials to my vitae), but in my research, as well. I quickly picked up new—at least, for me—methods of doing rhetorical analysis, my favorites being critical cartography for imagining spatial and mobile dimensions of rhetorical ideas and the usage of the Text Encoding Initiative (TEI) standard for encoding text-based historical materials. My dissertation work began to pick up momentum, as I dreamed of tacking on a final chapter with a digital component that would move my project beyond the traditional textual format—which would have been a first for my department. (Ultimately, I couldn't convince my advisor that it was worth the extra time and effort before I defended in 2017, less than a year after I officially began my work with AADHum.)

Ironically, but honestly, I was both part of AADHum's staff and a member of its target audience. I was a part of the community I was working to build, and on most days, it did not feel like work. It felt as though I was simply showing up to learn, even if I had had a hand in crafting the syllabus for the day. Being part of AADHum brought with it invaluable gifts that I had never before experienced in my young academic career: consistent access to robust, intellectually challenging conversations that centered non-white thinkers and theorizing; an obvious boost in my own scholarly motivation and production; hands-on skills training in emerging and innovative methods of research and engagement; a social environment that prioritized caregiving and emotional returns; and, a steady, life-supporting paycheck.

That's not to say that I did not succeed in my role. In the span of two and a half years, I was promoted from Graduate Assistant to Postdoctoral Associate and finally to Assistant Director. While I continued to leech off of AADHum's programming for my intellectual and professional benefit, my main contribution was in administration. True, I had spearheaded AADHum's foray into under-graduate education and pedagogy, the other major area of my academic passion, but the bulk of my work involved keeping track of the everyday. I authored a majority of AADHum's messaging; I kept our social media accounts and website updated; I coordinated events and initiatives among our guest speakers, visiting scholars, and community members; I organized information and data; I designed surveys; I scheduled meetings and check-ins and enforced deadlines. I checked things off lists. I did not find it taxing or difficult; I'm good at administration. If I'm being my most truthful, I always felt like I took more from AADHum than I gave.

That's why it was so strange to me how it all ended, even though, in hind-sight everything aligned perfectly and predictably. In spring 2019, as the news of AADHum's success in securing a second round of grant funding trickled down the chain of command, I was also slowly realizing that none of my colleagues on AADHum's staff were talking about sticking around. I started to listen more closely and pay attention to what I never had to know before—that the dynamics surrounding AADHum's infrastructure and personnel had come to a head, and no one that had truly steered this ship was being asked to stay on board.

Except me.

How could that be? Catherine, our strong, insightful, caring, visionary leader, was headed back to the Department of Communication to earn the tenure that was already rightfully hers. She had taken a half-formed thing and made it entirely whole in ways no one else could have envisioned or predicted; she breathed life into the pages of a grant proposal and imagined a future for Black DH communities that would grow and evolve as dynamically as Black history and culture has. Jovonne, our master of all trades, our intellectual polyglot and powerhouse, had facilitated every productive conversation and forum AADHum ever hosted. AADHum managed to talk successfully across interdisciplinary boundaries because of her, because she never failed to remind us—and then teach us how—to speak to the living, breathing folks in the actual room in ways that invited others in, too. Yet, Jovonne was already planning for a future that would not only take her away from AADHum but away from the region alto-gether. Kevin, whose relationships with different departments and units across campus charted a path for AADHum to move in groundbreaking ways, was headed into his dissertation defense without the next step in place. The logis-tics of our events, our promotional campaigns, even our office furnishings—he had simply made it all happen, sometimes seemingly by magic. Yet, there was nothing waiting for him at the end of it all. There was no mention, either, of what would happen to the two remaining Graduate Assistants, William Thomas and Melissa Brown. Everything was dissolving. Everyone was going their separate ways.

Except me.

Of the entire AADHum staff, I was the only one to receive a retention offer. And I was the only non-Black member of AADHum's staff.

There is a great injustice in that, but nothing surprising. AADHum, championed as a Black DH initiative unlike any other in its time, was subject to the same systems and structures of racism, white supremacy, and academic capitalism that it hoped to confront. Over the course of three years, but certainly, at its end, the labor of AADHum's Black staff was consistently undervalued and unrecognized. Without any discussion, justification, or any staff meeting with the new PIs, a new order was established: the people that built AADHum as a space for community, care, intellectual rigor, and inspiration were to be left behind and replaced with one person—me?

It became immediately clear that the same superficial "qualifications" that delivered me to AADHum in the first place were not a far cry from the reasons I was targeted for retention. I was still invested in Black scholarship, and I was still "tech-savvy." While I couldn't fathom how AADHum might continue without the staff that had built and nourished it or how AADHum might stay afloat without the people who supported its whole weight, I got the sense that the folks handing me the offer thought it to be perfectly reasonable. They thought the work of AADHum was what they *saw*, and from what they could see, I got things done. Visible things. Measurable things. Marketable things. I had proven that I could check off all the boxes that would make AADHum *look* like it was still AADHum. The program itself could be gutted—if even just temporarily— but at least the emails would still get sent, the social media accounts would still be active, and the events would be efficiently coordinated and executed. I knew enough to keep things running. Even without a new Director or any other staff in place, I could come back on board as Assistant Director and keep one hand on the helm of an empty ship.

My heart had already left, but old graduate-student habits die hard, and I had long been taught that any offer is a good one in the academy. I decided to negotiate the offer and demand reasonable compensation for the kind of labor they clearly valued; if I was to play host to the ghost of AADHum, I wanted a title and a salary that would indicate some recognition of what they had given up in exchange for what they were settling for. To put it crudely, I needed to be paid generously to attach my name to whatever AADHum would end up being once everyone who built it had gone.

They did not budge. (To be fair, they *said* they would improve the terms, but the final offer delivered 12 hours later did not reflect verbal promises.)

It was a deeply sad, heartbreaking goodbye to a program that I genuinely loved and felt so very proud to have played a small role in. It was even more disheartening to see the people I had grown so close to, the people I admired intensely, the people whose work and spirits had revived me be dismissed so unceremoniously. I will never forget how fortunate I am that, for a shining moment, I got to live the sort of academic life that so many others have been barred from. For just shy of three years, we made it happen—an "it" that would simply not have been possible with any other assemblage of people, aspirations, or talents. Maybe its end, then, was inevitable; we couldn't stay together forever, and it would not have been right for any one of us to stay in piecemeal.

So, we took our lessons and left.

Black DH projects should prioritize Black thinkers and scholars in hiring and retention. How else can Black DH continue to ground technical training and digital research in Black history and culture if Black folks are not leaders in the work? It's not enough for a Black scholar to be involved in grant writing or to maintain a ceremonial position of visibility at major events. Black DH centers and initiatives need to be imagined, led, directed, and staffed by Black people, with meaningful ties and investments in Black communities—locally, regionally, nationally, and globally—to build productive caregiving networks needed to sustain the work. The growth of Black DH as a field is an opportunity to carve out and hold intentional, supportive space for Black thinkers, researchers, and teachers in academic spaces that historically devalue and dismiss the contributions, experiences, and labor of Black people.

The institution will always take as much Black labor as possible, so give only until you've gotten what you came for. Black DH projects run on Black people's labor—the kind of work, creativity, care, inspiration, determination, sweat, courage, resourcefulness, good humor, and sass that have fueled Black history and culture for generations. And, Black DH as a field will continue to grow so long as scholars and researchers continue to invest their time, energy, and talent into its evolution. But the institutions who benefit from this work—in funding, in prestige, in diversity accolades—have yet to develop and sustain real mechanisms for recognizing, rewarding, and compensating the Black people who carry whole initiatives on their backs. Remember this hard truth, and be sure that you are forging your own path toward ends that are meaningful to you. Set honest and realistic goals: do you want to complete a research project with the support of the program's resources? Do you want to connect with a network of scholars in an adjacent field? Do you want to master a certain skill set to procure a desired position? Do you want to establish a presence within your community that will allow you to do different kinds of work? Be intentional about your own goals and remember it is not your responsibility to do it all. Sometimes being honest about your own objectives means leaving room for those that will come next.

The work is about the people, or it ends. Black history and culture has never been the work of just one, or a few, but the collective many—and the same holds true for Black DH. Through AADHum, we learned that the life and energy of the initiative came from its people—from the participants eager to learn, the scholars who demanded more, and the staff who worked to hold it all together. It's easy to be tempted by offers and promises from institutions and funders, especially in a world where resources seem increasingly scarce. But it's not enough to go or stay where you are invited. Instead, it's perhaps more important to continually ask yourself: with whom do I truly want to share my gifts? Whom do I want my work to serve? When is it time to walk away?

Kevin: "The Spook Who Sat By the Door"

I came to the University of Maryland as an unfunded, non-declared graduate student from Southern Illinois University Carbondale. The promise of funding was never a given for me. Not only did I have to take what I could find, but my sources of funding often did not come through my department or even my college. Being an unplanned graduate student afforded me the opportunity to forge partnerships across multiple units of my university and to move behind and underneath the veil. I am reminded of Sam Greenlee's book-turned-movie, *The Spook Who Sat By the Door*. In it, there is a scene where the lead character, Dan Freeman, is training other Black operatives in the methods of government spycraft while leaning on the strategic advantages of being subjugated in the racial contexts and formations of the United States. He says, "Next stage of your training program is to learn how to steal. I know you're all experts in stealing from your Black brothers and sisters now. You will learn how to steal from the enemy. Remember, a Black man with a mop tray or broom in his hand can go damn near anywhere in this country and a smiling Black man is invisible." What I still hear in that quote is an understanding of subjugated epistemology. How do we take what is given to us—from knowledge traditions that are not always to our benefit—and reshape that knowledge for the communities that we hope to serve and represent? How do we use the cover of marginalization to do what we can, when we can?

My experience as a graduate outsider informs my understanding of academic institution building, whom it typically benefits, and at whose expense. It also gives me an understanding of its potential. In 2016, I parlayed my time and skills from my degree in marketing into a position with the Dean's Arts and Humanities Center for Synergy. The ARHU Synergy's mission was to help faculty, students, and the larger community make connections across the diverse yet interconnected disciplines of the college. With respect to my own intellectual future, I knew I needed to be connected to the newly announced AADHum initiative. However, the Dean's office, proxied by Sheri Parks and ARHU Synergy, was not in a position yet to make decisions on staffing. Our director, Catherine, had not been recruited at this point. To eventually work on the AADHum Initiative, I first agreed to work on "Baltimore Stories: Narrative and Life of an American City," a grant project funded by the National Endowment for the Humanities: Humanities in the Public Square. The project focused on using narratives to help promote empathy, understanding, and healing for a city that just endured major civic uprisings the year prior. The University of Maryland found itself navigating new contexts for community engagement; its mixed history with the city of Baltimore was growing increasingly complicated by issues of justice and equity in the wake of continued protests and state violence in the Black Lives Matter era.

While working on that project, I also had the privilege to witness behind-the-scenes debates about the AADHum initiative's future—like those that considered the challenges of recruiting a senior-level scholar in the field of Black digital studies and what compromises would be acceptable if they couldn't find someone working squarely at those intersections. The bodies in the room are important here, in this retelling. A Black woman and Co-PI, Sheri Parks, held firm that the person in charge must be a part of the Black Studies tradition. Another Black woman, our dean, had to wrestle with that premise and institutional expectations around rank. This tension of hiring someone "competent" *versus* hiring someone Black played out on all levels of planning, including conversations about my own value to the growing grant.

What could I—a DH outsider, and an outsider to my own department—bring to this initiative that one of MITH's veteran resident scholars and staff could not? The answer, in my opinion, was the reality that Black projects, and projects with explicit Black community missions, need Black project management. I brought an institutional refugee's epistemology to the work of project management. I understood where the loose resources were; could identify and connect with potential partners with extra funding; had learned to navigate the network of staff administrators across the university; and, was already familiar with the offices that are often ignored and the kinds of infrastructural knowledge that is rarely activated.

I brought the type of knowledge you learn when you try to survive an institution that never planned for you to be there. Or, as Tupac said, "cease and desist with them tricks, I'm just another black man caught up in the mix. Trying to make a dollar out of fifteen cents." This was the value I brought to the grant as its project manager. Yet, due to the bureaucracies of the process, I was still not hired onto AADHum in a just or affirming manner. I was hired for the project *before* the director. I was *given* to the director and the initiative. In this context, developing trust with a direct superior could have been a challenge. Having my ideas heard without bias or skepticism could have been an issue. However, our team's relationship was built with respect for our own individual beliefs in and commitments to the mission. For all of us, there were these micro-moments where the institution asked us to pick between immediate personal favor and the grant's primary directives. For me, that looked like deciding how I could use interpersonal knowledge for the benefit of the community, the grant team, or external administrative forces.

There was a running joke that, truthfully, was never a joke—that much of the logistical success of the AADHum was made possible by the connections I had and favors I called in to the administrative and blue-collar class of the institution. I forged social capital through intentional acts of community building, which could resemble acts of public acknowledgment of support staff's labor, bringing cookies to the dean's administrative offices on a weekly basis, or any number of other gestures in between. The objective was always relationship cultivation and acknowledging the additional labor we were asking of people. You would have had to take a careful look at AADHum's budget to realize that it was those relationships, that social and community currency, that allowed us the shiny things we had—like an affordable and portable multimedia studio that supported our social media and streaming platforms. The relationships I forged and carefully maintained even provided affordable access to furniture and technology for our AADHum office. It got us what we needed, when we needed it. We were able to provide improvements to the academic grant experience at every level of programming, research, and professional development. Like I said—it was never really a joke. No one ever laughed at AADHum's spook who sat by the door.

My time as a graduate student was synced to the grant cycle. My transition was natural. The people in charge knew I would be willing to stay for the right opportunity—one that more closely aligned with how my work as project manager should be paid and acknowledged. That opportunity was never given, and that is okay. By the time AADHum's first iteration ended, the various stakeholders we worked with—our institutional partners, our PIs, the people we worked alongside most intimately—were gone without fanfare. That hurt, but the message was clear. They were going in a different direction with the future of AADHum and we should have convinced junior faculty—a community of scholars who already have research agendas established—to add additional projects to their plans and celebrate them for doing so.

I am proud of the work we did. It was successful, and the community let us know our work had an impact that aligned with what we had intended. An academic community formed around our efforts and Black Digital Studies and Black DH had begun working toward a more successful merger. From special issues in *Digital Humanities Quarterly* to *Debates in the Digital Humanities*, we have seen explicit acknowledgment of the field and intellectual community. Scholars who have come through our program are getting hired to jobs with explicit Black-and-digital calls.

My time with the college's Center for Synergy provided me with universal lessons for directing and administering initiatives and centers at the college level. In the National Humanities Alliance Foundation's Humanities essay, "Goals for the Publicly Engaged Humanities," Daniel Fisher (2022) notes five common goals from which all centers operate:

1. Informing contemporary debates;
2. Amplifying community voices and histories;
3. Helping individuals and communities navigate difficult experiences;
4. Expanding educational access; and
5. Preserving culture in times of crisis and change.

ARHU Synergy's mission certainly fits within these operating principles. Yet, working with AADHum provided lessons beyond what I think I could have learned elsewhere.

When the institution tells you who they are through their actions, believe them. The end of my tenure with AADHum and with various other units at the University of Maryland came in 2019. This included the Arts and Humanities Center for Synergy. This center, the umbrella institution involved with our formation, rebranded itself as the Maryland Center for Humanities Research and shifted its priorities from community toward offering seed funding for faculty, lectures, and special programming. The change in their mission narrowed their audience to the faculty of the University of Maryland. Their mission changed. Mine did not. So when they told me that what I was there to do no longer aligned with their goals, I believed them. They wanted something different. That's okay. It's okay to move on when your goals no longer match those of the organization.

Privileging the mission is not privileging sustainability. Truthfully, there was a moment for each of us where we could have kept working for and with AADHum—or some version of it—but at what cost? Our desires for the initiative strayed too far from institutional objectives. To stay at AADHum would require us to realign with a new purpose. That was not our calling. We were fortunate enough to be prompted to check in with ourselves and one another. The life cycles of grants afford that opportunity if we are willing to take them. Accepting further funding without using the respites between cycles for serious reflection is a mistake I'm glad we didn't make.

So you have a hit record. Okay. Go make another one. Sometimes you just have to know your talent. Toot your own horn and recognize you have the ability to replicate the things you create. When circumstances require you to pick between your calling and preserving the status quo, it is okay to choose what feels right. We are all still actively pursuing the mission to create a community for those not often included at the intersection of digital. We are alright. Catherine has the Black Communication & Technology Lab (BCaT); Jessica is the interim director of Design Cultures & Creativity; Jovonne is Senior Program Officer for Higher Education Initiatives at the American Council of Learned Societies; and I have gone on to be part of the founding team for two other Mellon-funded Black digital projects: the Center for Black Digital Research and the Project on Rhetorics of Equity, Access, Computation, and Humanities (PREACH) Lab at Georgia Tech University.

Walking Away

When we look back at the sum of our experiences, we acknowledge that our stories can read as depressing. When our local team and community of scholars dissipated, we felt like we failed. Without the programming and the physical space for students and faculty to gather, what would become of the fellowship we built during those years? Yet, in putting together this text, we needed a framework to reaffirm that our conscious decisions to follow an ethic of love and to operate with radical intentionality, were not a mistake. We needed to find a way to be okay with the consequences of our decision to walk away. This led us back to Black cultural traditions and alternative forms of epistemological validation. Instead of defining success in terms of sustainability or continuity of a grant, we refocus our attention on the continuity of practices in radical intentionality that spilled out into our larger intellectual fellowship in Black DH. In shifting our goals away from the temporal nature of the grant cycle and toward the long life cycle of developing a field, we give ourselves permission to walk away—again.

Clyde Woods (1998) points toward a Blues epistemology as a mechanism for survival and resistance. The Blues is a culture that transcends place and connects people based on their common experiences of oppression and their beautiful imagination about the future. Using the Blues as a metaphor, Woods details the importance of sitting with the pain of the past, requiring accountability in the present, and imagining a more beautiful future. Detailing and documenting the life and work of Black folks in the U.S. by singing and studying the Blues provides us a lens for our experiences in doing Black DH with radical intentionality. We used this text to sit with the reality of what we hoped to do, what we ultimately did, and how we've pursued accountability for the ways that both individuals and institutions might negotiate external markers of success and the practical needs of marginalized communities.

Many institutions are sincere about wanting to address the growing desires of students and faculty to build structures to support Black DH research on their campuses. Acquiring grants to create faculty lines and create new centers is a laudable goal. Yet, even with these ideals at the forefront of our collective minds, every project team and every institution will confront a plethora of systemic issues that push the objectives and goals of major grants out of alignment with the communities they are first imagined to serve. We navigated this reality, and we've considered what it means to walk away—to imagine a future apart from the work we created in the present. We've endeavored to do as Woods suggests, to "explore the subterranean caverns that shelter the wellsprings of dreams during the seasons when hope can't be found" (Woods, 2009, p. 430).

Historically, Black musicians formed groups to support themselves, get music deals and gigs, and provide safety as they traveled. However, these musicians were rarely tied to a single band permanently. New Orleans artists were often involved in multiple jazz ensembles with numerous exponential combinations of members. As the situation dictated, the bands would dissolve and (re)form based on the needs of the musicians and the community. As they relocated, formed new groups, and played new music, they learned new skills and created new sounds—all the while surviving and acquiring the necessary resources to continue to play. Sometimes, on some nights, the groups "failed," but the band played on. For this team, we learned that drafting the radical values was the easy part; being okay with the consequences of those values leading to "failure" was quite another. Ultimately, the end of the story for this team carries the lesson of how a strong and impactful program with ample resources and funding can—and perhaps *should*—fall apart so that it can begin anew.

In the end, we came together and then departed, on the basis of our own values, not those of the institution. Our commitment to radical intentionality continually motivated us toward three goals we each carry forward for the next stages of Black DH in our own lives and careers: first, in doing Black DH, we must always center on the Black people doing the work and who will benefit from the work; second, we will continue to decenter and disrupt the tools in order to engage intentional critiques of the impact of technology on the lives of Black people; and third, the future of Black DH is in community building.

Without intentionality, it is possible to retain funding but impossible to sustain a community. Take the affirmation from the communities you choose to represent and, if the system changes—or shows itself to be ever the same—that's okay. Stepping away not only allows us to do what we are meant to do, what we are equipped to do; it also makes room for other folks to step in and do the work, bring new energy, discover new harmonies, and explore different sounds.

As Jay-Z says, "You made a hit, go make another one."

References

Fisher, D. (2022). Goals of the publicly engaged humanities. *Humanities For All*. https://humanitiesforall.org/essays/goals-of-the-publicly-engaged-humanities

Woods, C. A. (1998). *Development arrested: The blues and plantation power in the Mississippi Delta* (Ser. Haymarket series). Verso.

Woods, C. A. (2009). Katrina's world: Blues, bourbon, and the return to the source. *American Quarterly*, *61*(3), 427–453.

APPENDIX A

WE WHO WOULD BUILD

Re-visioning Resistance and Theorizing Beyond the Gaze

Jovonne Bickerstaff

Reprinted with permission (originally published on the AADHum blog 2017)

> We have two hands: one is to battle, one is to build. We battle. We resist by calling out threats to our dignity by name. We build. We actively protect our dignity by creating what works. Those two hands may be on one person, one organization may be set up to do both. For others, they are the battling or the building kind. Either way, the battlers need the builders. The builders need the battlers. This is a discipline of resistance.
>
> —*Brittany Packnett, activist*

Outlining her concept of "Black studies in the wake," Christina Sharpe emphasizes its call "to be at the intellectual work of a continued reckoning the longue of Atlantic chattel slavery, with black fungibility, antiblackness ... accounting for the narrative, historical, structural, and other positions black people are forced to occupy." Drawing on Alexander Weheliye, Kim Gallon, by contrast, characterizes Black Studies as "a mode of knowledge production" that "investigates processes of racialization with a particular emphasis on the shifting configurations of black life."

Building on the Duboisian tradition of intellectual activism that advances scholarship while furthering social justice, both suggest that the real and vital work on black people necessarily speaks to race—that is, analyzing the consequences of and resistance to the project of racialization.

I can see how interrogating the racial project of whiteness that shapes black folks' lives can be a way of speaking truth to power for African Americanist scholars. Still, focusing so acutely on unpacking racism and racialization as sole or primary path of resistance gives me pause. I wonder if we've framed what Black Studies does—and more importantly can do—too narrowly.

Might our pre-occupation with black struggle, whether in the conditions of or resistance to oppression, make us complicit in the diminishing the fullness of black humanity and what we might explore in it? Can we imagine examining black experience without making America's racialization project the dominant idiom?

Recently, activist Brittany Packnett developed a Twitter thread which began, "We have two hands: one is to battle, one is to build." Certainly, we African Americanists know how to battle. So much of our training as scholars prepares us for it; we're socialized to privilege the work of critique and deconstruction. Given how black folk have been conceptualized or written out of cannons, our proclivity towards confrontational debate may be more pronounced. We feel the pulse of that resistance when Gallon characterizes Black Studies as "the comparative study of the black cultural and social experiences under white Eurocentric systems of power." But ... is that enough? Is our conception of black scholarly resistance too narrow? Taking Packnett's call for a multifaceted strategy of resistance to heart, I must ask, when do we build?

These questions are central to who I've become as a scholar. Surely, I do my share of confrontational resistance, interrogating problematic paradigms, particularly when I teach. Still, as my research agenda solidifies, I'm more compelled by that call to build. Centering black experience has been my entry point for moving beyond critique to imagine new narratives and inquiry to engage in what I term theorizing beyond gaze—orienting my own work and my hopes for the AADHum Initiative.

> From my perspective there are only black people. When I say "people", that's what I mean ... No African American writer had ever done what I did ... even the ones I admired ... I have had reviews in the past that have accused me of not writing about white people ... As though our lives have no meaning and no depth without the white gaze. And I have spent my entire writing life trying to make sure that the white gaze was not the dominant one ... I didn't have to be consumed by or concerned by the white gaze ... The problem of being free to write the way you wish to without this other racialized gaze is a serious one for an African American writer.
>
> —*Toni Morrison*

Freedom for her, Nina Simone once quipped, was the absence of fear. As a scholar and writer, my vision of freedom is more akin to Toni Morrison's and begins with one radical tool: choice.

I name, frame, and lay claim to different terrains: examining understudied populations (couples in enduring relationships), raising novel questions (how emotional strategies for resilience impact intimacy), and situating my research in unorthodox literatures (sociology of emotions vs. "the black family"). In every case, each she/he/they that I describe is, by default, black. Refusing to explicitly qualify race in work on black people can be jarring because having non-white experiences centered is so rare. In addition to disturbing notions of black folks as the perpetual other, theorizing beyond the gaze forces us to recognize how failing to fully account for positionality undermines our theorizing.

If we uphold confrontation as the primary or most effective tool of resistance, I fear we risk neglecting how resistance requires and has always relied as much on subversive tactics like theorizing beyond the gaze as on direct action. In the AADHUM initiative, I hope that helps us think through how can we begin to construct a "meaningful intellectual and activist challenge" that circumvents the analyses of injustice that re-isolate the dispossessed, à la McKittrick's invocation of Gilmore.

It'd be easy (and reductive) to see black Twitter simply as an off shoot of mainstream Twitter use. But what if we saw it instead as innovation narrative, à la Steve Jobs and iPods and iPhones, whereby they're responsible for optimizing technology use in ways that reveal its fullest potential? Or conversely, could we invert the arrows of co-optation, which typically focuses on stolen American products, to reveal how communities of color used Twitter and Vine towards subversive ends of mobilizing social change (i.e. BLM), celebrating black joy in the mannequin challenge or viral memes on Vine?

Ultimately, how, when and why we enter as African Americanists, seems to turn largely on who we are working for and what we are working towards. The aim is not to abandon the battle, but simply to recognize that, while necessary, it is insufficient.

My hope in the AADHum Initiative is that we move towards what Brittney Cooper calls "liberatory world-making"—imagining new ways of seeing and thinking about that intersection of digital studies and African American research. We battle and we build … and we choose the work to which we'll devote our hands each day. Today, I build.

APPENDIX B

EXCERPTED SYLLABUS FOR FIRST YEAR RESEARCH INTENSIVE COURSE

Digital Archives

Course Description

> …liberatory archives are not things so much as they are processes. Understanding them, then, is not a 'what' question as much as a 'how' question.
>
> —*Jarrett M. Drake*

This course is the first in a two-semester research stream in African American Digital Humanities: Digital Archives, which builds on the core work of the African American History, Culture, and Digital Humanities Initiative (AADHum). For Black and African Americans, whose voices have historically been silenced in traditional institutional archives, digital spaces can provide an opportunity for creative expression and argument that challenges dominant narratives. Situating itself at the intersections of African American history, rhetoric, and digital humanities, this research stream aims to develop a book project—and, later, a supplementary interactive website—that considers how Black and African Americans create and engage in digital spaces that resist oppression, centralize Blackness, and argue for freedom.

Students will first become critical analysts of public discourse and its preservation in traditional archives. Then, students will be challenged to contribute a chapter to the book that amplifies and digitally preserves Black people's arguments for and about *freedom*. During *weekly class meetings* and approximately *6 hours of independent research per week*, students will learn practices for conducting critical research in archives, acquire skills to build their own digital archives, and cultivate the critical sensibilities to explore how digital practices can have lasting consequences for social change.

Learning Outcomes

General Education Distributive Studies, Humanities Course Outcomes

This course broadly studies history and genres of human creativity. Upon completion of this course, students will be able to:

1. Demonstrate familiarity and facility with fundamental terminology and concepts in a specific topical area in the humanities.
2. Demonstrate understanding of the methods used by scholars in a specific field in the humanities.
3. Demonstrate critical thinking in the evaluation of sources and arguments in scholarly works in the humanities.
4. Describe how language use is related to ways of thinking, cultural heritage, and cultural values.
5. Conduct research on a topic in the humanities using a variety of sources and technologies.
6. Demonstrate the ability to formulate a thesis related to a specific topic in the humanities and to support the thesis with evidence and argumentation.

Discipline Specific Learning Outcomes

Additionally, this course aims to develop students' capacities in communication research, especially rhetorical analysis, as well as skills and methods in digital humanities. Upon completion of this course, students will be able to:

1. Conduct communication research by identifying problems, crafting substantive research questions, producing rhetorical analysis of discursive texts, and formulating informed arguments.
2. Communicate and participate actively in teamwork and collaborative research and sharing their work in both written and oral formats.
3. Identify and analyze public discourse shaping African American history and culture.
4. Apply methods for digital research and analysis, including collecting and organizing textual data, transcription, text encoding, and web design.
5. Exhibit personal and professional autonomy by anticipating and independently navigating research problems.

Learning Outcomes by Assignment

Assignment	General education outcomes	Discipline specific outcomes
Research Deliverable 1: Reading Questions (Parts 1 and 2)	GE1, GE2, GE3	DS1
Research Deliverable 2: Research Proposal	GE5, GE6	DS1, DS3, DS5
Research Deliverable 3: Proposal Presentation	GE4, GE5, GE6	DS2
Independent Research Log (Part 1)	GE1, GE2	DS2, DS5
Research Deliverable 4: Literature Review	GE3, GE5	DS3
Research Deliverable 5: Digital Edition	GE2, GE5	DS4, DS5
Research Deliverable 6: Digital Archive Presentation	GE5, GE6	DS2, DS4
Independent Research Log (Part 2)	GE1, GE2	DS2, DS5
FIRE174 Survey	--	--
Participation/Discussion	GE1, GE4	DS2

Required Materials

No textbook is required for this course. All readings will be made available via electronic means, under Fair Use copyright provisions, in our Canvas coursespace. *You are expected to learn how to navigate our Canvas coursespace, access class materials in advance of deadlines, and come to class meetings prepared to engage in reflection and conversation.* While you are generally encouraged to be environmentally responsible in your printing habits, you are more than welcome to bring hardcopies of the readings to class meetings and lab hours if referring to the texts will help you (1) contribute actively and meaningfully to discussion/skills practice, and/or (2) take more effective notes.

Four free, open-source software programs are required for this course: Atom, GitHub Desktop via the GitHub Student Developer Pack, Tropy, and Zotero. Download and installation guides are available in our Canvas coursespace. Please be sure to download all four programs to your preferred electronic devices and become proficient with their operation. In the event of a technical issue that prevents you from acquiring these programs, please let me know immediately.

Assignments and Grading Policies

Assignments. Our research progress throughout the semester will be assessed by several benchmarks, for which brief explanations are provided below. Further direction will be offered both in class and with comprehensive, detailed rubrics.

- **FIRE174 Survey**. At the end of the semester, all students participating in FIRE courses will be asked (via email) to complete a brief survey about their experience. Students will receive points for completing the survey.
- **Independent Research Log (Parts 1 and 2)**. Students are encouraged to devote approximately 6 hours per week to independent research, which will ultimately contribute to the development of the research stream project. Students will be provided with a research log template, which they must update on a consistent basis with details about goals, tasks, challenges, and accomplishments. (While roughly 6 hours will be needed per week to suitably accomplish recommended research tasks, each student is encouraged to work at their own speed to complete their work. Our shared focus will be on *progress*, rather than pace.) Research logs will be submitted and graded at mid-term and again at the end of the semester.
- **Research Deliverables**.
  - *Reading Questions.* At the start of the semester, students will be introduced to the book project by engaging with relevant theory and literature in African American history, culture, and digital humanities. To begin developing their research instincts, each student will develop meaningful questions that identify, critique, sustain, and/or advance key problems animating these fields.
  - *Research Proposal.* Each student will propose an independent research project that will form the basis of a chapter in the larger book project. The proposal must (1) *identify*, *assemble*, or *create* an appropriate collection of texts for analysis; and (2) include a well-crafted research question with the potential to intervene in both academic and public conversations about *freedom* for Black people. Research questions should be specific, identifying a rhetorical problem or possibility that arises in the collection; thoughtful, considering how such a problem or possibility is significant to nuanced understandings of freedom; and practical, presenting the feasibility of rhetorical analysis and digital preservation of the collection.
  - *Proposal Presentation.* Presenting your ideas and soliciting feedback is crucial to the research process and the development of compelling ideas. As such, students will present their research proposals to their peers in an informal talk, during which they will (1) share initial observations about the collection's scope, significance, and key rhetorical features; (2) answer questions and invite feedback regarding their research question, initial analysis, and potential research challenges; and (3) discuss the implications of digital preservation for their chosen collection.
  - *Literature Review.* Each student will situate their research project within a history of *freedom* ideas. Students will identify and draw upon 8–10 primary sources and supplementary secondary scholarship to animate either (1) a specific era with rhetorical parallels to their collection, or (2)

a progressive arc of historical events or conversations that illuminate the significance of their collection. These literature reviews should emphasize the ways in which *freedom* discourse is being revisited, redressed, and/or redefined through digital practice.

- *Digital Edition*. Students will learn how to preserve traditional and born-digital documents using text encoding. Following the Text Encoding Initiative (TEI) standard, students will create a digital edition of a single text from their chosen collection. Students will interrogate encoding practices by actively centralizing Black people and Black voices in their work and will justify their encoding choices and rationale with thorough documentation.

- **Digital Archive Presentation**. At the culmination of the semester, students will showcase skills in transcription, text encoding, and web design by completing and presenting a digital archive. Each student will use GitHub to build and publish a multi-page website, which will include digital editions of each text in their chosen collection; documentation of their encoding choices; excerpted adaptations of their Research Proposal and Literature Review to frame the archive; and a full bibliography. Each digital archive should clearly demonstrate the focus, significance, and early analysis of a single book chapter in a larger project devoted to understanding Black *freedom* in digital discourse.

- **Participation/Discussion**. Students' active contributions to discussion and skill-building will be assessed throughout the semester. In addition to being physically present, students are expected to contribute meaningfully to the research experience by asking questions, providing feedback, and participating in activities. Of note: these expectations are not meant to impose an undue burden on your physical, mental, or emotional health. If you have concerns about how your unique mode(s) of participation will be assessed, please do not hesitate to let me know as early in the semester as possible.

Revisions. If you wish to improve the quality or content of a submitted assignment★ for any reason, you are welcome to revise and resubmit within 14 calendar days of the original assignment deadline. Please be advised that a revision submission involves a full re-assessment of an assignment. A revision does not necessarily guarantee a *higher* grade. ★*Note*: All revisions must be received at least 3 days prior to the semester's final grading deadline.

Research Calendar

Readings and assignments are listed *on the day that they are due and/or are to be discussed. This schedule is subject to change, depending on our needs. All changes will be discussed and deliberated as a team.*

Date

1/30

Focus

We'll discuss the syllabus and the research project, briefly reviewing its roots in questions of humanity, freedom, and the history of ideas.

Readings and Assignments/Recommended Independent Research Tasks

- Prepare for the semester by downloading, installing, and familiarizing yourself with the required open-source software.
- Carefully review the Course Syllabus again. Take note of questions of concerns you can share at our next meeting.
- Visit the National Archives. Use the National Archives catalog to search for records housed at the College Park location, and that may be of interest/relevance to you and this course. Then, use NARA's website to help you prepare for your visit to the College Park location. When you visit the archives: first, take detailed notes regarding the various rules and practices that govern traditional archival research and access; second, take notes about the research you conduct there (e.g. what records did you look at? What did you find? What is interesting or important about them?); third, preserve your work by taking digital photos of archival documents and organizing them using your Tropy software.

Date

2/6

Focus

Archives of Freedom. We'll assess practices of power and privilege in traditional archives and archival research. Students will draw on their own experiences in the archives and learn vital research practices—especially locating, evaluating, and citing primary source material.

Readings and Assignments

- Jessica H. Lu, excerpt from *Reckoning with Freedom* (2018)
- Saidiya Hartman, "Venus in Two Acts," *Small Axe* (2008)
- Marisa J. Fuentes, "'Venus': Abolition Discourse, Gendered Violence, and the Archive," *Dispossessed Lives* (2016)
- Research Deliverable 1a: Reading Questions, Part 1

Recommended Independent Research Tasks

Explore and contribute to an online transcription project. Consider, for example, the Smithsonian's National Museum of African American History & Culture or Freedmen's Bureau collections, or the Newberry Library's Civil War in Letters transcription project. Take detailed notes that summarize what you did to prepare for and contribute to the transcription project; reflect on the implications of the transcription process for reading, analyzing, and understanding histories; discuss the possibilities and problems presented by the digitization of archival texts.

Date

2/13

Focus

Digital Archives: Possibilities and Problems. We'll consider the implications of digital archives. Students will identify digital material that publicly (re)negotiates freedom and demonstrates the potential for resistance and reimagination in digital spaces.

Readings and Assignments

- Catherine Knight Steele and Jessica Lu, "Defying Death: Black Joy as Resistance Online," from *A Networked Self* (forthcoming)
- Michelle Caswell, "Inventing New Archival Imaginaries," from *Identity Palimpsests* (2014)
- Jarrett M. Drake, "Liberatory Archives," Parts 1 and 2 (2016) OR "I'm Leaving the Archival Profession" (2017), *Medium*
- Research Deliverable 1b: Reading Questions, Part 2

Recommended Independent Research Tasks

- After our regular class meeting, we'll attend Jarrett M. Drake's Digital Dialogue, "Repositories of Failure: Creating Abolitionist Archives to Project Past the Punishment Paradigm," from 12:30 to 2:00pm in 0301 Hornbake Library (MITH Conference Room). Students who are unable to attend must watch the livestream recording.
- Take stock of your own digital worlds by closely examining the discourse that textures your online experience. What kinds of conversations are you seeing, hearing, and/or participating in? Whose Black voices are being amplified, and in what ways? Whose voices should be amplified more meaningfully? How is freedom being negotiated, contested, or celebrated in striking ways? Be prepared to identify 2 or 3 digital spaces and/or conversations that pique your interest.

Date

2/20

Focus

Conceiving the Research Project. We'll navigate the process of conceptualizing and developing a research project by identifying specific texts and/or conversations that can be digital preserved and critically analyzed. Students will learn how to craft specific, thoughtful, and practical questions that can sustain a research project, as well as intervene in broader humanities conversations.

Readings and Assignments

- Sarah Florini, "Tweets, Tweeps, and Signifyin'," *Television & New Media* (2013)
- Catherine Knight Steele, "The Digital Barbershop," *Social Media + Society* (2016)
- Bergis Jules, "We're All Bona Fide," *Medium* (2018)
- Read about the DocNow project

Recommended Independent Research Tasks

- Prepare your Research Proposal.
- As you conceive your project, search for other studies in African American history, culture, and digital humanities that may serve as productive models. Reading other scholars' research will help you think through your own ideas and processes.
- Visit Jessica during office/lab hours to discuss your potential project.

Date

2/27

Focus

Conceiving the Research Project (cont'd).

Readings and Assignments

Research Deliverable 2: Research Proposal.

Recommended Independent Research Tasks

- Prepare your Proposal Presentation. Remember to practice your presentation at least several times, and develop a list of likely questions you may be asked to address.
- Visit Jessica during office/lab hours to practice your presentation.

Date

3/6

Focus

Conceiving the Research Project (cont'd).

Readings and Assignments

Research Deliverable 3: Proposal Presentation.

Recommended Independent Research Tasks

- Having completed your research proposal and presentation, begin to chart the landscape of the conversation you're entering. Who has written about your topic and what did they say? Locate and read pertinent scholarship (journal articles, book chapters, blogs, digital projects). If possible, find relevant scholars, writers, and project makers online (i.e. Twitter and professional websites) and tune into what they're saying. Be prepared to identify several ways in which your project will respond to or advance the conversation.
- Finalize your Independent Research Log in preparation for your Part 1 submission.

Date

3/13

Focus

Defining Context and the Politics of Citation. We will immerse ourselves in the history of ideas that contextualize contemporary freedom discourse. Students will learn how to trace ideas through public language practices and define a rhetorical context for analysis.

Readings and Assignments

- Robin James, "A Non-Zero Sum Game," *It's Her Factory* (2017)
- Explore the #citeblackwomen and #amplifypoc hashtags on Twitter
- Independent Research Log, Part 1

Recommended Independent Research Tasks

- Begin to outline and write your Literature Review. As you do so: first, get in the habit of saving and organizing your sources using Zotero; and second, catalog your reasons for citing particular scholars, speakers, and thinkers. Take note of the ways in which you are defining the shape, scope, and texture of history.

• Be sure to rest, as much as possible, during your Spring Break!

Date

3/27

Focus

Creating Digital Surrogates via Text Encoding. We will use markup software and text encoding to digitally preserve public discourse and interrogate the possibilities and problems of digital archives. Students will be introduced to Atom text editor and the Text Encoding Initiative (TEI) standard to create a Digital Edition based on one of their chosen texts.

Readings and Assignments

• Explore the TEI website
• Read the Atom Flight Manual

Recommended Independent Research Tasks

• Dive deeply into the TEI Guidelines to familiarize yourself with encoding basics and language. Which types of modules and elements are you most likely to use when encoding and analyzing your own collection? Learn more about them.
• Revise and finalize your Literature Review.

Date

4/3

Focus

Creating Digital Surrogates via Text Encoding. (cont'd)

Readings and Assignments

Research Deliverable 4: Literature Review

Recommended Independent Research Tasks

Practice your TEI header markup with the supplied examples. Craft a header for three different *types* of documents. Attend an AADHum Digital Humanities Incubator in the Social Movements module. See Jessica for date/time/location details.

Date

4/10

Focus

Creating Digital Surrogates via Text Encoding (continued)

Readings and Assignments

* Jessica Lu, "Confronting 'the Witness': Encoding Archives of Black Lives," AADHum Blog (2017)
* Hannah Gillow-Kloster, "TEI: Affordances and Restrictions" and "Editing and Decision-Making", Digital Orlando

Recommended Independent Research Tasks

Extend last week's practice by encoding each example's text body.

* Develop a system for thoroughly documenting your encoding choices and rationale.
* Be prepared to share your digital surrogates with your peers, for comparison and discussion.
* Visit Jessica during office/lab hours to troubleshoot encoding problems and uncertainties.

Date

4/17

Focus

Creating Digital Surrogates via Text Encoding. (cont'd)

Readings and Assignments

None!

Recommended Independent Research Tasks

• Work on, revise, and finalize your Digital Edition. Ideally, your Digital Edition should serve as the model for your other digital surrogates.
• Be sure to devote appropriate time to developing thorough documentation.
• Visit Jessica during office/lab hours to troubleshoot encoding problems and uncertainties.

Date

4/24

Focus

Building a Multi-Page Website Using GitHub. We will store and manage our digital editions online. Students will learn how to create and publish a multipage TEI website using GitHub and GitHub Desktop, and will use basic HTML and CSS coding skills to build their digital archive.

Readings and Assignments

• Complete the "Hello World2 GitHub Tutorial
• Research Deliverable 5: Digital Edition

Recommended Independent Research Tasks

• Having completed your first Digital Edition, move on to encode the remaining texts in your collection.
• Continue to document your encoding choices and rationale, and visit Jessica during office/lab hours to troubleshoot encoding problems and uncertainties.
• At the same time, practice using GitHub and GitHub Desktop to create a static website from your digital edition(s). Follow your instructor-supplied guides multiple times to familiarize yourself with the GitHub process.

Date

5/1

Focus

Building a Multi-Page Website Using Github (cont'd).

Readings and Assignments

Search the internet for basic HTML and CSS tutorials

Recommended Independent Research Tasks

- Finalize the content of your digital editions.
- Build and style a multi-page GitHub Site, adding introductory copy (adapted from your earlier Research Deliverables) that frames the digital archive in terms of critical analysis and the history of freedom ideas.
- Prepare and practice your presentation.
- Finalize your Independent Research Log for your Part 2 submission.

Date

5/8

Focus

Presenting Research. We will share the work we have completed during the semester. Students will further develop their communication skills by presenting their digital archives to their peers for feedback.

Readings and Assignments

- Research Deliverable 6: Digital Archive Presentation
- Independent Research Log (Part 2)

APPENDIX C

AADHUM INCUBATOR MODULE 3 SESSION 1

Movement of People

AADHum Module 3: Movement of People

Session One

Start Time	Duration	Description
2:00	2 minutes	Welcome; any general AADHum updates
	2 minutes	Participant intros
2:05	15 minutes	Intro to Module 3: Theme
		Objective: What about movement of people into and around PG county makes it ripe for humanities geospatial work? What are the kinds of questions and evidence
		• Focus on internal migration
		• Focus on intra-regional migration
		• Post-"Great Migration": 1968 as Prologue (ref dc1968 project)
		• Discussion/exercise: Ask participants to generate a list (shout out) what kinds of things might be significant to studying migration, e.g. "jobs", "where is transit?", "where are other people like me?"
		• How to study migration from a cross-disciplinary humanities perspective that is not (only) importing social science methods
		• Representation and self-representation—how did PG county come to see itself as a "Black place"

Start Time	Duration	Description
2:20	15 minutes	Discussion • Prompt: Three short clips on Landover Mall (1972 ad, go go performance, interview with bookseller) • Mary Sies and possibly GAs from Center for Global Migration Studies will be attending—let's take advantage of their expertise in an informal way

2:35	5 minutes	Intro to Module 3: Arc of these 4 sessions
		• Enumerate what each session will cover in brief—like the blurbs on the flyer
		  • Sessions 2: How do we see and identify in space markers of "African American culture"?
		  • Session 3: How do we do geospatial analysis (versus "just" mapping)
		  • Session 4: How do we use new analytical methods to understand changes in self-representation of PG county?

2:40	15 minutes	Refresher on Map Skills *Objective: why are we remembering these particular skills?* • Georeferencing • Layers • Raster • Vector
2:55	5 minutes	Focus of map skills for this module: from narrative/illustrative maps to geospatial analysis—asking questions of our maps • "God's eye"-view versus point-to-point or zones of knowledge "on the ground" • Show one or two examples of "demographic" maps and talk about how they encode information?
3:00	10 minutes	Introduction to QGIS • Where does it come from? • Why is it open source? • What can it do?
3:10	5 minutes	Introduction to PostGIS • PostGIS builds on PostgreSQL? What's PostgreSQL? • What's SQL? • What does PostGIS add? • Thinking about geo information in terms of queries • Exercise: Participants shout out/generate a list—what kinds of queries can I have about geo information?
3:15	10 minutes	QGIS Cloud • Cloud QGIS Server and Database • Explain how it helps

Start Time	Duration	Description
3:25	5 minutes	Where do we go next • Tee up session 2 • Point to ELMS site
3:30		End

INDEX

Pages in *italics* refer to figures and pages followed by "n" refer to notes.

For Product Safety Concerns and Information please contact our EU
representative GPSR@taylorandfrancis.com
Taylor & Francis Verlag GmbH, Kaufingerstraße 24, 80331 München, Germany

www.ingramcontent.com/pod-product-compliance
Ingram Content Group UK Ltd.
Pitfield, Milton Keynes, MK11 3LW, UK
UKHW021447080625
459435UK00012B/396